T0274927

Tautonyms: tautonyms

TAUTONYMS:

tautonyms

by
Michael J. Stephan

Illustrations by Rob Rex

Foreword by Jon Reidy & Guha Krishnamurthi

For information on ordering, updates, and future editions, please contact the author at mjstephan@gmail.com.

Illustrations by Rob Rex. Foreword by Jon Reidy & Guha Krishnamurthi. Cover designs by Michael J. Stephan.

ISBN: 979-8-35091-075-9

Some authors having found difficulty in selecting generic names which have not been used before, have adopted the plan of coining words at random without any derivation or meaning whatever. . . . Such verbal trifling as this is in very bad taste, and is especially calculated to bring the science into contempt. It finds no precedent in the Augustan age of Latin, but can be compared only to the puerile quibblings of the middle ages. It is contrary to the genius of all languages, which appear never to produce new words by spontaneous generation, but always to derive them from some other source, however distant or obscure. And it is peculiarly annoying to the etymologist, who after seeking in vain through the vast storehouses of human language for the parentage of such words, discovers at last that he has been pursuing an ignis fatuus.

—Report to the British Association for the Advancement of Science by committee appointed to develop rules of zoological nomenclature, 1842.

CONTENTS

TABLE OF ILLUSTRATIONS

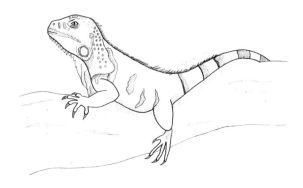

Iguana iguana

Special acknowledgment is given to Rob Rex,
a wonderful friend of many years and the illustrator of this book.

FOREWORD

WHAT'S IN A NAME? "THAT which we call a rose by any other name would smell as sweet,"[1] but the deaths of literature's most famous young lovers—and the very existence of this book—belies the dismissal of a name as something which can be separated from that which it identifies. Words matter. From our very birth, those that should love us most anxiously await our first spoken words. While we are conditioned in the earliest stages of socialization that "words can never hurt me," we intuitively recognize at a very young age the fallacy of such wishful thinking. And throughout our lives we use words in innumerable forms to execute and express every facet and stage of the human condition. Words are art. Words are science. Words matter.

And so it is with nomenclature of the animal world. *Tautonyms* is an exploration of the deep history and process of how we identify animals and why. Its examination of the often descriptive, always purposeful nomenclatural process elucidates the deep connection animal names have with the animal form.

An oft-repeated maxim in the philosophy of acting, attributed to the great Russian thespian Konstantin Sergeyevich Stanislavski, holds that "there are no small parts, only small actors." Science is much the same. In his deft production of *Tautonyms*, Michael J. Stephan has demonstrated a depth of commitment equal to any researcher in contributing to the scholarship of bedrock science. And it is a commitment which never halts, and never falters in rising to meet the rigors of truth.

---

1   WILLIAM SHAKESPEARE, ROMEO AND JULIET, act II, scene II (1597).

In the *Tractatus Logico-Philosophicus*, Wittgenstein declared, "The limits of my language mean the limits of my world."[2] In *Tautonyms*—whether in methodically collecting tautonyms, pellucidly explicating various scientific names, or meticulously tracking their etymologies—Stephan has, in a Wittgensteinian conception, *literally* expanded the boundaries of our world of human experience. There are no small advances in knowledge, only small minds. Consider also the transitive value of nomenclature. The entire human experience is informed, enhanced, and indeed enabled by science. We needn't be coy: Our existence is begat by science. Science itself depends on nomenclature. Ergo, our existence—life itself—depends on nomenclature.

America didn't go to the Moon because it was easy, but because it was hard.[3] *Guernica* wasn't frivolity, it was compulsion. And Stephan hasn't birthed *Tautonyms* fully formed from his head like Athena from Zeus because words don't matter, but because his compulsive pursuit of scientific excellence demanded no other result in this timeline. Do not mistake *Tautonyms* for a subtle gasp in the cacophony of science. It's Gabriel's Horn. A thunderclap in the desert of nomenclatural literature. It is no less than Promethean, a *Heavenly Spheres* for the 21st century.

The best Christmas Carol adaptation is The Muppet Christmas Carol—in large part because two-time Oscar winner Michael Caine plays Ebenezer Scrooge against a bunch of puppets like he's playing King Lear on the London stage. However the conceit of Muppets doing Dickens might appear, Caine never behaves like he's among puppets. He gives the material

---

2   LUDWIG WITTGENSTEIN, TRACTATUS LOGIGO-PHILOSPHICUS (1922). The precise meaning of this has been an enduring question (and perhaps the polymath Stephan will summit that mount next).

3   JOHN F. KENNEDY, ADDRESS AT RICE UNIVERSITY ON THE NATION'S SPACE EFFORT (Sept. 12, 1962) ("We choose to go to the moon in this decade and do the other things, not because they are easy, but because they are hard, because that goal will serve to organize and measure the best of our energies and skills, because that challenge is one that we are willing to accept, one we are unwilling to postpone, and one which we intend to win, and the others, too.").

and the movie the effort and the gravitas it deserves—his utmost. And his performance and the movie itself are all-time classics as a result. *Tautonyms* might appear as fanciful as Dickensian puppets, but it will outlive us all. Treat it like Shakespeare.

Jon Reidy & Guha Krishnamurthi

PREFACE

What is the difference between a dead skunk in the middle of the road and a dead lawyer in the middle of the road?

There are skid marks in front of the skunk.

IN A LETTER TO EVOLUTIONARY biologist Richard Dawkins three years ago, I jokingly compared lawyers to skunks and rhetorically asked whether I might have been happier in my life by pursuing a career in the study of roadkill skunks than in the study of law. That got me thinking: *What is the name for a person who studies skunks?* The answer to this question led to another question: *Where does the word "mephitologist" come from?* Each question's answer prompted a new question until I had spent a considerable amount of my evening reading about the Samnite goddess of foul-smelling gasses and the concept of tautonyms.

I was surprised to learn that tautonyms are rare. Of the 1.8 million living organism species that are estimated to have been described, around 1 million to 1.5 million are animals, and of those, only a few hundred appear to have tautonymous names—at least according to then-existing lists of tautonyms. Given the relatively small universe of tautonyms and my interest in animals and etymology, I decided to build my own list of tautonyms. My list would be more extensive than, but reliant upon, existing lists, and it would provide something new: a brief description of each animal and an explanation of the etymology of its scientific name.

Initially, I did this purely for my own amusement with no plans of sharing my research publicly. As I amassed around 200 or 300 entries and friends convincingly feigned interest in this project, I decided that my efforts had reached a tipping point and that I ought to memorialize this research in some permanent place. This book is that place.

The task of completing this research has been a tiring one. I was tempted to end the project when its difficulties became too great, and nobody would have noticed if I had. It is the arbitrary and self-assigned nature of this work that made it especially hard to push through the challenges that arose. Why should I spend hours reading ancient texts about the hump-nosed viper with no assurance that the origins of this animal's name will become any clearer, or that the origins, if discovered, would be of interest to anyone but me? Why spend half a day translating French and Russian only to link a monastery in the Gulf of Finland to a flatworm? I don't have good answers to these questions, but there is something rewarding about being able to confirm the etymological origin of a name that was previously unknown to me, and perhaps, to everyone except the person who invented the name. Still, there were moments—even shortly before publishing—where I discovered some trove of twenty or thirty *or a hundred* additional tautonyms of some poorly documented and uncharismatic animals that I knew would take weeks to unravel. I questioned whether this whole thing is worth the effort.

For all its difficulties, this project has also caused me to learn a great deal about the world I inhabit. In a way, this project has taken me on a brief but unusual tour through time and across many civilizations and continents. I have become more familiar with a variety of foreign languages and cultures, and I now know more about parasitic worms, moths, and the skin-incubation of Surinam toads. I am a real hoot at parties.

As discussed in the Introduction, the topic of this book is trivial and should not be taken too seriously. I am not formally trained in the relevant subject matter and the importance of this research to the world is questionable. While some friends have helped me with proofreading, any errors or omissions in this book are my own. As with any scientific or reference text, I also expect to discover new tautonyms just 0.2 nanoseconds after my final manuscript is printed, making a second edition or online supplement necessary to satisfy my completionist nature.

I am grateful for the people who encouraged me to pursue this project over the years. Some of you are zoologists that kindly tolerated my many questions. Some of you are friends and family that patiently nodded along to my untethered ramblings about taxonomic history. Some of you are strangers who, like me, have an inexplicable interest in the arbitrary yet amusing quirk of scientific language that is explored in the pages that follow.

Michael J. Stephan
May 2023

PART I:

INTRODUCTION

Mephitis mephitis

THERE ARE FEW SUBJECTS MORE arbitrary and less important than tautonyms. This is why no effort has been made, until now, to publish a comprehensive list of all tautonyms in the animal kingdom with detailed etymological explanations for them and descriptions of the animals to which they refer. To many readers, this book may therefore offer little more than a catalogue of largely useless information and a memorialization of the time wasted by its author, who is neither an etymologist nor a taxonomist by trade.

That said, seemingly trivial information sometimes captures our curiosity in ways that traditionally valuable facts about the world do not. Entire books are published, year after year, detailing "useless information," including that peanuts can be used to make dynamite and that 83% of people struck by lightning are men. So why shouldn't we also have a reference book dedicated to the relatively rare occurrence of an animal having a scientific name that is a single word repeated? Indeed, tautonyms have been the subject of taxonomic discussion for over 180 years and modern magazines occasionally feature pop-science articles that provide short lists of tautonyms, which suggest that tautonyms have some permanence in scientific and popular culture.

The pages that follow tell the story of this oft-neglected subject, which lies at the intersection of wordplay, etymology, and wildlife biology. In many ways, this book may provoke one's imagination about the relationship between humans and other members of the animal kingdom as many scientific animal names reflect historically important events, ideas, behaviors, and myths of our human ancestors. Moreover, this book's selection criterion for animals is tautonymous names—a more or less random occurrence often caused by historical accident or the unpredictable whims of zoologists. As a result, the animals profiled represent a slice of the vast biodiversity found on this planet. Tautonyms are not limited to any one continent, habitat, timeframe, or taxon. They include birds of the Arctic tundra, harvestmen of the Brazilian rainforest, and catfish of southern Asia. They include creatures big and small, extinct and extant, classified long ago and only recently. Finally, this book may also provide wildlife enthusiasts and logophiles with an introduction to the science of taxonomy, a field less glamorous than others but vital to wildlife conservation efforts. If we are going to identify and protect threatened species, we first need to define them in taxonomic terms.

It is in naturally curious people that this book will find its audience, and it is in this book that such people may find something more than a mere string of facts. Readers are encouraged to reflect not just on the formation of tautonymous names, but on the formation of all names, and to push the scholarship on tautonyms and other peculiarities of science and language to new heights. There are few subjects more arbitrary and less important than tautonyms, yet it is in the overlooked frontiers of arbitrary and unimportant subjects that the soil of discovery is the richest.

Part I of this book provides background information on the definitions, scope, and methods for this project. In Parts II through IX, tautonyms and their potential etymologies are set forth, organized roughly by taxonomic rank of class or phylum. Bibliographical information and an appendix are provided in Part X.

WHAT IS A TAUTONYM?

A tautonym is a scientific name in which both parts of the name have identical spelling. For example, the striped skunk is a member of the *Mephitis* genus and its specific name is *mephitis*, making its scientific name *Mephitis mephitis*. Tautonyms can be formed when animal species are named for the first time, or when they are reclassified and given new scientific names.

For a tautonym to occur, the spelling must be identical in both the generic name and the specific name. For instance, the scientific name of the meerkat is *Suricata suricatta*. This name is not tautonymous because although the generic and specific names are nearly identical, they are slightly varied. It is also not a tautonym when both parts of the name are different words that share a common meaning. This is known as a pleonasm and would include names like *Ursus arctos*, where both words mean "bear" in Latin and Greek, respectively. There are many others, including *Felis catus* and *Ovis aries*. A scientific name need not have identical capitalization to be a tautonym. Scientific naming conventions dictate that generic names begin with capital letters and specific names begin with lowercase letters, and tautonyms are formed when the two words are spelled the same regardless of those capitalization differences.

A subset of tautonymous names are tautonymous trinomials, meaning the generic, specific, and subspecific names are all identical. The scientific name of the Canada striped skunk subspecies, *Mephitis mephitis mephitis*, is one example. Others include *Bison bison bison* (the Plains bison), *Cardinalis cardinalis cardinalis* (a subspecies of the northern cardinal), and *Vulpes vulpes vulpes* (the Scandinavian red fox). Tautonymous trinomials are perhaps more common than one might think. Subspecies division itself is fairly common, and according to rules of zoological nomenclature, the classification of sub-species always results in a nominate subspecies being named. In other words, every tautonymously named species that has a subspecies also has a tautony-mous trinomial subspecies. While this book does not provide an exhaustive list of tautonymous trinomials, it mentions them on occasion and provides a list of mammal tautonymous trinomials in the Appendix, where a list of the major taxonomic ranks and other miscellaneous information is included.

This book focuses on animal names, but it is worth noting that the rules of nomenclature for algae, fungi, and plants expressly forbid tautonyms (and discourage pleonasms) when naming such organisms. There are, however, near-tautonyms in the botanical world, including *Ziziphus zizyphus* (the common jujube) and *Salacca zalacca* (the salak palm). There are also former, now-invalid tautonymous names for plants including *Lablab lablab* (the hyacinth bean, currently classified as *Lablab purpureus*), *Opuntia opuntia* (the eastern prickly pear, currently classified as *Opuntia humifusa*), and *Thevetia thevetia* (the yellow oleander, currently classified as *Cascabela the-vetia*). Rules of nomenclature for bacteria previously prohibited tautonyms, but that restriction was removed from the bacteriological rules in 1975. A detailed history of the tautonym rules for these other biological groups can be found in the Appendix.

Finally, there are many animals that once had tautonymous names but that have been reclassified and now have non-tautonymous names. This includes *Polyspila polyspila* (the leopard ladybug), which is currently clas-sified as *Calligrapha polyspila*. In an effort to provide a complete account of the tautonyms in the animal kingdom throughout time, this book includes former tautonyms as well as current tautonyms, indicating where tautony-mous names are no longer considered valid or were never considered valid. For inclusion on the list that follows, a tautonymous name need only to have appeared in at least one reliable scientific or quasi-scientific source. Obvious typographical errors of names by non-scientific sources are not included (*e.g.*, "*Hydrochaeris hydrochaeris*" appears to be a common misspelling for the capybara, *Hydrochoerus hydrochaeris*). That said, some of the tautonyms included herein are rather dubious, even for invalid names, and have been noted as such.

WHAT IS A SCIENTIFIC NAME?

For the purposes of this book, scientific names of animals are defined as binomial names published in scientific descriptions on or after January 1, 1758. This date is widely considered the starting point for zoological nomenclature because it was in 1758 that Carl Linnaeus published the tenth edition of his *Systema Naturae*, which was the first work to consistently use binomial nomenclature across the animal kingdom. Binomial nomenclature is the standard in zoological nomenclature today, and a binomial name consists of two parts: a generic name (*Tyrannosaurus*), and a specific name (*rex*). Binomial nomenclature is also essential to the formation of a tautonym, which has two ("bi-") names ("nomen") that repeat.

Prior to publication of the tenth edition of *Systema Naturae*, most zoological catalogues used polynomial names for animals. These polynomial names sometimes look like binomial names, but are often significantly longer and appear more like short Latin descriptions rather than unique labels. Polynomial names were even used in pre-1758 versions of *Systema Naturae*, which is why the main date of priority is fixed to the publication of the tenth edition.

The date that is fixed to the definition of "scientific names" is important because it means that tautonyms created before that date will not be listed in this book. There are quite a few potential tautonyms that appear in scientific literature before 1758, but that are excluded from this book because they were not necessarily binomial names and therefore cannot be assessed under the same criteria as binomial names published in 1758 or later. Over 90 such names appear in Linnaeus's first edition of *Systema Naturae*, published in 1735. A list of those names and more information on their formation is provided in the Appendix.

It is also important to distinguish scientific names from common names. For instance, the native Barombi name for a small fish species in a lake in western Cameroon is "myakamyaka," sometimes written as "myaka myaka." This name has two parts that are identical, arguably making it a tautonym. It does not appear as a tautonym on this list, however, because it is a common name and not a "scientific name." Specifically, it is not a binomial name published in a scientific description in 1758 or later. Having said that, the native Barombi name formed the etymological basis of the scientific name that was later assigned to this fish in 1972, and this fish's current scientific name is the tautonym, *Myaka myaka*.

WHERE ARE TAUTONYMS RECORDED?

There is no single list of all tautonyms, near-tautonyms, or former tautonyms. People unfamiliar with taxonomy might also be surprised to learn that there is no single list of all animal species that are known to exist or to have existed. There are not even complete lists of all known mammals, reptiles, fish, birds, or insects. Incomplete lists of these different animal types are abundant, but there is no one definitive and complete source that can be laboriously reviewed for tautonyms.

For the most part, the recording of animal descriptions and species names is done in scientific research papers and books, which may sometimes be flawed, incomplete, outdated, or preempted. Indeed, confusion in research papers—including misspellings and misidentifications—are sometimes responsible for creating tautonyms. But even when research is complete and accurate, there is no assurance that any particular scientific name assigned in a research paper will make its way onto a public list or database of similar animals.

The lack of reliable lists of all known animal species makes the task of identifying all tautonyms nearly impossible. There are simply too many animal species names—roughly 1 million to 1.5 million—that are not organized in a centralized resource, which prevents one from saying with confidence that any list of tautonyms is complete. Although this book is probably the most thorough collection of tautonyms to date, it almost certainly omits some relatively unknown but legitimate tautonymous names. Moreover, the classification and naming of animals is ever-changing. A non-tautonymous crown wasp today might be reclassified and given a tautonymous name tomorrow. The fossilized remains of a previously undiscovered Pacific newt or Malaysian green lacewing might be found next week and described for the first time with a tautonym.

The tautonyms in this book have been gathered from a variety of sources, including existing but incomplete tautonym lists. Special acknowledgment is given to Samuel S. Long and Mark Isaak for their early efforts to collect many of the tautonymous names that are provided herein. Long pioneered "tautonym-collecting" and observed that unlike rock-collecting and coin-collecting, tautonym-collecting is clean, requires little exertion and storage space, and does not deal in items of value: "I don't have a safe to keep my tautonyms secure, nor do I have to pay anyone when I come across a tautonym." Notwithstanding the ease and inexpensiveness of the activity, few have attempted it, which adds to the challenge of finding all tautonyms in the animal kingdom. Even Long's list of tautonyms, while impressive and no doubt the culmination of months or years of work, is not even half of the animal names provided in this book.

In addition to existing lists, helpful researchers in a variety of zoological fields have provided tautonyms that they came across in their own research. Other methods for finding tautonyms included reviewing complete lists of all taxon names created by naturalists who appear to have had a habit of creating tautonyms. One such example is entomologist William Harry Evans, who created thousands of taxon names for lepidopterans, many of which appear in this book. Another example is malacologist Felix-Pierre

Jousseaume, who is responsible for over 50 mollusk tautonyms. Yet another (admittedly unscientific) method for finding tautonyms was simply intuitive research as to where tautonyms might likely be found and conducting a time-intensive manual review of thousands of species names within select orders or families. There is no perfect method for finding tautonyms, but at well-over 600 species, the list presented here is at least inclusive enough to be considered the leading list and worthy of memorialization.

WHAT METHODS ARE USED TO DETERMINE ETYMOLOGICAL ORIGINS?

Determining a name's etymological origin is often not a straightforward matter. It requires understanding not only the meaning of the name and the object that it is assigned to, but also the intent of the person assigning the name and the language from which it came. Unfortunately, this information is often missing from our historical records. Words—both written and spoken—change over time as people use them in new ways and in different languages. An early name for an animal might be used to describe one species or ten similar species. The reason or intent behind a name is rarely recorded and is often not obvious.

Modern species descriptions tend to provide etymological explanations of scientific names, but this practice did not become commonplace until relatively recently. For the first 200 years or so of Linnaean-inspired taxonomic classification, many naturalists would simply assign a name to an animal with a short description of its appearance and habitat—nothing more. Before Linnaeas formalized zoological nomenclature in the mid-18th century, naming conventions were even more disorganized and inconsistent. For these reasons, it can be difficult to conclude why a particular brown skipper that looks indistinguishable from thousands of others is named *Joanna joanna* without more information.

Where possible, every proposed etymology in this book that was not unambiguously explained in the original animal description has been checked against multiple sources, including etymology books and websites, foreign language dictionaries, and books on scientific word composition. The phrase "proposed etymology" is intentional as many of the etymologies provided are little more than educated guesses and should be understood as such. It is simply an unfortunate fact that some etymological origins have been lost to history or were never properly understood in the first instance, particularly where animal names are based on seemingly random letter arrangements, anagrams, or other unknown whims of their authors. American zoologist Theodore Gill captured the spirit of this challenge: "The means for ascertaining or confirming the etymologies of many scientific names are, perhaps, not available for all who might desire to ascertain them, and they are often wrongly analyzed."

The opening quotation of this book, taken from one of the earliest attempts to memorialize rules of zoological nomenclature, likewise describes the etymological frustrations caused by "nonsense names" and other words of indiscernible origin. Such names included words formed "at random without any derivation or meaning whatever," like *Xema*, *Quedius*, and *Spisula*, as well as anagrams of other names like *Dacelo* and *Cedola* of the name *Alcedo*. These names were so despised that they were once considered "objectionable" by zoologists and their use was strongly discouraged. That is no longer the case. Such names have now been allowed for well-over a century, and many of them are tautonyms included in this book. As that 1842 zoological committee explained, these names are "peculiarly annoying to the etymologist, who after seeking in vain through the vast storehouses of human language for the parentage of such words, discovers at last that he has been pursuing an *ignis fatuus*."

Accordingly, the proposed etymologies herein should be viewed as likely, or highly likely, and not definitive. Where a name's etymological origin is less clear, the description of the name will use an adverb like "probably" or "presumably," or will state outright that the origin is unclear and that there is little information upon which to make a reliable guess. Even in those instances where the etymology is unclear, creative etymological analysis is provided to prompt the reader's imagination as to what the name might mean. It is possible that including speculative etymologies of this type will ultimately do more harm than good to this book's credibility, but a thoughtful reader should appreciate the many limitations and caveats now articulated.

In most instances, any non-English words that form the bases for scientific names are provided using the English alphabet without diacritics or other special symbols. This includes words in Greek, Latin, Tupi, Japanese, Bengali, French, Russian, Proto-Indo-European, and many others. Every effort has been made to use internally consistent and reasonably understandable letters to accurately reflect non-English words in the appropriate case and gender, although this is not always feasible.

Where different sources provide alternative etymologies for a single name, both explanations are provided. Etymologies will be revised in future editions should new information become available, and readers are encouraged to offer corrections and suggestions.

WHAT OTHER INFORMATION ABOUT TAUTONYMS IS AVAILABLE?

In addition to etymological information, the entries that follow include English common names, basic descriptions, and interesting facts for each animal. This book is not an encyclopedia and is not intended to provide granular detail about the bubblenests of armored catfish. The information provided is intended to give a general sense of what the animal is, usually with a mention of its distribution or habitat. With some exceptions, regional descriptions that include compass directions tend to use attributive adjectives rather than attributive nouns to avoid implying that animal distributions are confined by the political boundaries often associated with attributive nouns (*e.g.*, "southern Asia" instead of "South Asia"). Sometimes, descriptions go into lengthy detours about animal behavior, mythology, or other topics for no particular reason and without warning. To borrow a phrase from English poet Samuel Taylor Coleridge, who once compared his writing style to the tautonymously named *Pipa pipa*, "My thoughts bustle along like a Surinam Toad, with little toads sprouting out of back, side, and belly, vegetating while it crawls."

Reasons why animals were given their names are provided, though these are also subject to some level of speculation and should be understood as not conclusive. Note that the reason why an animal might be given a name is different from the plain meaning of the word or words that make up the name. The saucereye porgy's scientific name, *Calamus calamus*, seemingly comes from a Greek word for "reed," but it is unclear whether the reference is to the aquatic reed plants where young saucereye porgies make their homes, or to the hollow, reed-like spines on their anal fins. The armored catfish, *Callichthys callichthys*, provides a good example of how different characteristics of an animal can give rise to different explanations of a single name based on different potential source languages.

Although tempting, this book will not provide the history of binomial nomenclature, the reason for scientific names to take Latinized forms, or the reasons why there are so many lepidopteran and coleopteran species on this planet. These subjects are covered in many other superior resources for an interested reader to explore. This book also will not provide the names of the zoologists who first described each species, the years in which each species was classified or reclassified, or the history of priority and synonymity of each scientific name. That information is not always necessary in zoological publications, but it is publicly available for anyone who wishes to dive deeper into the history of a particular scientific name.

On the topic of Latinized forms, it is sufficient to say that Latin and Ancient Greek had the advantage of being widely understood and accepted by European scholars of the 18th century when zoological nomenclature was becoming standardized. Accordingly, references herein to Greek are generally to a Greek dialect of classical antiquity, rather than to modern Greek. On the topic of common names, if an animal has no recognized English common name, then the phase "no common name" will appear, although the animal might have a common name in some other language.

Finally, some interesting and related subjects worthy of books in their own right concern the roles of taboo replacement and folk etymology in animal names. Taboo replacement occurs when an animal is not called by its name because of a superstitious belief that saying the name aloud will cause something bad to happen. For instance, bears were once feared as dangerous beasts by ancient inhabitants of Eurasia, so instead of calling them by their name (a Proto-Indo-European word thought to resemble "hrtkos"), they were called something like "bear," meaning "brown one," or "medved," meaning "honey eater." Similar things also happened with wolf and fox species. The fear was that by saying the so-called "true" name of a ferocious animal, you would call it forth when you were not prepared for it. Another animal name taboo relates to animals like fish or deer that were hunted. The superstition was that if you say aloud the "true" name of an animal that you are hunting, it may hear its name and thereby know that it is being hunted. Similar superstitions exist today in the form of "knocking on wood" and phrases like "speak of the devil," "god forbid," and feeling "jinxed." Folk etymology refers to popular but false etymological explanations, and to words that change in form or meaning to be more familiar to the user. The scientific names of the killer whale (*Orca orca*, formerly) and the wolverine (*Gulo gulo*) are examples of each, respectively.

* * *

With those many explanations, limitations, and warnings out of the way, one can finally embark upon the long list of animal tautonyms and their potential etymologies that follows, but not without first enjoying one more apt excerpt from the 1842 zoological nomenclature committee's report to the British Association for the Advancement of Science:

We have now pointed out the principal rocks and shoals which lie in the path of the nomenclator; and it will be seen that the navigation through them is by no means easy. The task of constructing a language which shall supply the demands of scientific accuracy on the one hand, and of literary elegance on the other, is not to be inconsiderately undertaken by unqualified persons. Our nomenclature presents but too many flaws and inelegancies already, and as the stern law of priority forbids their removal, it follows that they must remain as monuments of the bad taste or bad scholarship of their authors to the latest ages in which zoology shall be studied.

Like that of the nomenclator, the rocks and shoals in the path of this tautonyms project have now been pointed out. The task of identifying relevant species and discerning the origins of their scientific names is by no means easy and should not be inconsiderately undertaken, but it has nevertheless been attempted here. Though this book may contain its share of flaws and inelegancies, with any luck it will stand as a monument, not to bad taste and bad scholarship, but to the marriage of literary elegance and scientific accuracy found in that unique form of taxonomic wordplay, the tautonym.

PART II:

MAMMALS

Nasua nasua

MAMMALS ARE VERTEBRATE ANIMALS GENERALLY characterized by having mammary glands that produce milk for nursing their young, fur or hair, three middle ear bones, and a neocortex. The mammal tautonyms identified below include seven bat species—a significant number that is perhaps not surprising given that bats make up roughly one-fifth of all known mammal species. The list also includes two extinct kangaroos, one of which (*Nombe*

nombe) was reclassified and given a tautonymous name in 2022 following new discoveries concerning the animal's teeth.

Alces alces — **moose.** The moose, known as an elk in Eurasia, is the largest and heaviest extant species in the deer family. The scientific name comes from the Latin word "alces," which came from the Proto-Germanic word "elkh" or "elho" for this animal. The original meaning of the Germanic word is unclear, but sources suggest that the word may refer to the reddish-brown color of the animal's fur (from the root "el-") or to the animal's strength (from the Greek goddess "Alke" personifying battle-strength and courage). The common name "moose" is derived from the Proto-Algonquian "mo swa," meaning "it strips," in reference to how a moose strips tree bark when feeding. Confusingly, the word "elk" in North America refers to a completely different species, *Cervus canadensis*. Early European explorers in North America called *Cervus canadensis* "elk" because of its size and resemblance to familiar-looking elk like the red deer of Europe.

Anoa anoa — **lowland anoa.** This species of buffalo is endemic to Sulawesi. It is small, standing barley over 35 inches at the shoulder and weighing between 330 and 660 pounds. It has been classified as endangered since the 1960s, due in part to habitat loss and hunting. Its scientific name is the Malay name for the animal in Sulawesi. This species no longer has a tautonymous name and is currently classified as *Bubalus depressicornis*.

Axis axis — **chital deer.** Also known as the spotted deer, the chital is native to India and known for its distinctive white spots on reddish-brown fur. The common name "chital" comes from the Hindi word "cital," which is itself derived from the Sanskrit word "citrala" meaning "spotted." The common name of the large cat species "cheetah" (*Acinonyx jubatus*) has a similar origin. The chital deer's scientific name "axis" is harder to trace. The earliest recorded usage of "axis" is from Pliny the Elder's *Historia Naturalis*, where he describes "a wild beast called the axis, which has a skin like that of a fawn, but with numerous spots on it, and whiter." It is unclear who, according to Pliny, called the animal the "axis." Pliny further identifies the axis as a "terrestrial animal of India," which provides another clue as to the word's potential origin. "Axis" might have come from the Sanskrit word "aksah," meaning "eyes," and would be a reference to the deer's many small, white spots, which could be perceived to vaguely resemble human eyes.

Barbastella barbastella — **western barbastelle bat.** This European bat is medium-sized with dark hair, broad ears, and a pug-shaped nose. Its scientific name is said to come from the Latin words "barba" for "beard," and "stella" for "star," apparently in reference to the white hairs that grow beneath its lower lip. This often-repeated explanation appears correct in its translation of Latin words, but it is questionable whether this bat's scientific name is actually a combination of "barba" and "stella." Another explanation is that the Latin word "vespertillum," meaning "bat," eventually became "pipistrello" in Italian due to assimilation of "v-" and "p-" sounds. This word was then modified by replacing "pipi-" with "barba-" to refer to the beard that this species appears to have when viewed from the side. Over time, "barbastrello" transformed into "barbastella" or "barbastellus." This bat is considered vulnerable or critically endangered in various parts of its range due to habitat loss, and several European countries have passed legislation to protect its habitats. This species no longer has a tautonymous name and is currently classified as *Barbastella barbastellus*.

Bison bison — **American bison.** The American bison, also known as the American buffalo, is a species of bison that once roamed North America in vast herds. The word "bison" comes from the Latin word "bison" meaning "wild ox." The word was borrowed from the Proto-Germanic "wisand-," which possibly came from Baltic or Slavic language terms for "the stinking animal" in reference to its scent while rutting. The American bison was nearly made extinct in the 19th century by a combination of commercial hunting and the introduction of bovine diseases from domestic cattle. From a population in excess of 60 million in the late 18th century, only 541 individuals remained by 1889. Conservation and recovery efforts in the mid-20th century fueled a population resurgence to roughly 31,000 wild bison today.

Capreolus capreolus — **roe deer.** Also known as the European roe deer and the western roe deer, this species of deer is widespread in Europe. Its scientific name is derived from the Latin word "capra" or "caprea," meaning "goat." The common name "roe" is thought to come from a Proto-Indo-European root, "rei-," meaning "streaked, spotted, or striped." This may be a reference to roe deer fawns, which are typically born with spots. Male roe deer are polygamous. During courtship, when the males chase the females, they often flatten the underbrush, leaving behind areas of the forest in the shape of figure eights called "roe rings."

Caracal caracal — **caracal.** This medium-sized wild cat is native to Africa, the Middle East, central Asia, and arid areas of Pakistan and northwestern India. Its name comes from its Turkish name, "karrah-kulak" or "kara-cou-lac," meaning "cat with black ears." The caracal is also known as the desert lynx and the Persian lynx, although present-day lynxes are in a separate genus that contains its own tautonymously named species (*Lynx lynx*).

Chinchilla chinchilla — **short-tailed chinchilla.** Both the scientific and common names for this endangered species of South American rodent come from the Spanish name for this animal. The origin of the Spanish word, "chinchilla," is less clear. One source states that it refers to the Chincha people of the Andes, who incorporated this animal's dense, velvet-like fur into their clothing. According to that explanation, the animal's name literally means "little Chincha." Other sources state that the name means "little bug," and is a diminutive form of the Spanish word "chinche," meaning "bug."

Chiropotes chiropotes — **red-backed bearded saki.** This South American monkey gets its scientific name from the Greek words "kheir" for "hand," and "potes" for "drink." This monkey drinks from the back of its hand by soaking the fur in water and licking it.

Citellus citellus — **European ground squirrel.** This rodent can be found in central and southeastern Europe. It is currently considered endangered because its population appears to have diminished by more than 30% over the last ten years, apparently due to loss of habitat. Its scientific name is the Latin word for a ground squirrel. This species no longer has a tautonymous name and is currently classified as *Spermophilus citellus*. The current generic name comes from the Greek words "sperma" and "philos," meaning "seed lover."

Congruus congruus — [**no common name**]. This extinct semiarboreal kangaroo existed in Australia during the Pleistocene epoch. Its scientific name comes from the Latin word meaning "congruent" or "agreeable," in reference to the fact that many of its cranial characteristics are similar to those of other members of the Macropodinae, which is a subfamily of marsupials in the family Macropodidae.

Cricetus cricetus — **common hamster.** The scientific name of the common hamster is a Latinized version of the Italian "criceto," meaning "hamster." It likely originated from the Czech word "krecek," also meaning "hamster." Where abundant, the animal is considered a farmland pest, and has also been trapped for its fur. It has declined drastically in recent years, likely due to habitat destruction, and is considered critically endangered. Other common names of this species include the Eurasian hamster and the black-bellied hamster.

Crocuta crocuta — **spotted hyena.** The spotted hyena, also known as the laughing hyena, is native to sub-Saharan Africa. The scientific name was once thought to be derived from the Latin word "crocutus," meaning "saffron-colored one," in reference to the color of the animal's fur. This is now understood to be incorrect, as the correct spelling of the word would have been "crocata," and the word was never used in that sense by contemporary sources. Rather, "crocuta" is ostensibly derived from the Greek word "krokottas," which comes from the Sanskrit word "karataka" (or possibly "kroshthara"). Through accidental inversion and confusion of letters, the word likely transitioned to something like "karakata," then "krakata," then finally "krokotta." The original Sanskrit word "karataka" comes from the word "krus," meaning "to cry," and refers to the golden jackal (*Canis aureus*), a wolf-like dog found in

Asia that is known for its unusual howling sounds. Subspecies include the tautonymous trinomial *Crocuta crocuta crocuta* and the extinct cave hyena, also known as the Ice Age spotted hyena, *Crocuta crocuta spelaea*.

Dama dama — **fallow deer.** The scientific name "dama" is a Latin word referring to animals of the deer kind, including roe deer, gazelles, and antelopes. In Croatian and Serbian, the name for the fallow deer is "jelen lopatar," meaning "shovel deer," in reference to the shape of its antlers. The word "fallow" comes from Old English and means "brownish yellow." The fallow deer was distributed mainly in the Middle East during the last ice age, but over the last two millenia human involvement has expanded the distribution of this deer by introducing it to Europe, Australia, North America, and South America.

Feroculus feroculus — **Kelaart's long-clawed shrew.** The scientific name for Kelaart's long-clawed shrew is a Latin word meaning "small and wild" or "small and fierce," presumably in reference to the animal's small size and spirited disposition. The common name of the species refers to zoologist Edward Frederick Kelaart, who described many plants and animals in Sri Lanka, where this long-clawed shrew can be found. This shrew is the only species within its genus, making the genus monotypic.

Fossa fossa —**Malagasay civet.** This small, nocturnal mammal is endemic to the tropical forests of Madagascar. It has the appearance and movements of a small fox and is the second largest carnivore in Madacascar after the fossa (*Cryptoprocta ferox*). It has a short grey or beige coat with dark black stripes and a bushy tail. It is also known as the striped civet and the fanaloka. Its scientific name comes from "fossa" or "foussa," the native name for this civet. This species no longer has a tautonymous name and is currently classified as *Fossa fossana*.

Gazella gazella — **mountain gazelle.** The mountain gazelle gets its name from the Arabic word "ghazal," meaning "wild goat." With the diminutive Latin suffix "-ellus," the name refers to a "small wild goat." Interestingly, the word "ghazal" also refers to a type of amatory Arabic poetry, and the word in its poetic sense is believed to have an etymological relationship to the word that refers to a gazelle. The poetic form "ghazal" potentially means something like, "the wail of a wounded deer," referring to the feelings of pain and loss that are often expressed in ghazal poetry. In many countries in northwestern sub-Saharan Africa, gazelle species are referred to as "dangelo," meaning "swift deer." Mountain gazelles were hunted throughout their native habitat in Israel because they were thought of as pests until 1993. Their numbers are still low for multiple reasons, and today they are considered endangered.

Genetta genetta — **common genet.** This small African cat has a long body, a ringed tail, and large ears. The origin of the word "genet" is unclear. It might have come from the Greek prefix "gen-," meaning "bear," and the Latin suffix "-etta," meaning "small." Alternatively, it might have come from the Arabic "jarnait" or the French "genette," referring to a civet-like cat. There are more than 30 subspecies of the common genet, including the *Genetta genetta genetta*.

Gerbillus gerbillus — **lesser Egyptian gerbil.** This rodent, also known as the pygmy gerbil or sand rat, gets its name from the Arabic word "jarbu," for "rodent." The diminutive Latin suffix "-illus" makes this a "small rodent." This species grows to a body length of about 3.5 inches with a tail of about 4.6 inches. By comparison, the greater Egyptian gerbil (*Gerbillus pyramidum*) has a body of 5 inches and a tail of 6 inches.

Giraffa giraffa — **southern giraffe.** The name "giraffe" has its earliest known origins in the Arabic word "zarafah." There are multiple explanations for where the Arabic word came from. One source states that it may have come from the animal's Somali name "geri." Another source states that it came from a compound of the Persian words for "flute" and "leg," in reference to the animal's long legs. The Arabic name is translated as "fast-walker." The modern English form developed around the year 1600 from the French word "girafe." The name "camelopard" has also been used to describe giraffes, with the northern giraffe being named *Giraffa camelopardalis*. The word "camelopard" comes from the Greek words for "camel" and "leopard" in reference to its camel-like shape and leopard-like coloration. The taxonomic classification of giraffes is subject to some debate, with some sources suggesting that this species is a subspecies of *Giraffa camelopardalis*. Others suggest that the southern giraffe is its own species with subspecies including *Giraffa giraffa giraffa*.

***Glis glis* — edible dormouse.** The word "glis" is Latin for "dormouse." The word "dormouse" probably comes from the Latin word "dormio," meaning "I sleep," referring to this animal's long periods of hibernation. It is called the "edible" dormouse because it was farmed and eaten by ancient Romans and Gauls, usually as a snack.

***Gorilla gorilla* — western gorilla.** The word "gorilla" comes from the history of Hanno the Navigator (c. 500 BC), a Carthaginian explorer on an expedition to the western coast of Africa to the area that later became Sierra Leone. Members of the expedition encountered "savage people, the greater part of whom were women, whose bodies were hairy, and whom our interpreters called Gorillae." It is unknown whether what the explorers encountered were what we now call gorillas, another species of ape or monkeys, or humans. The term was first used in binominal nomenclature in 1847 when the western gorilla was called *Troglodytes gorilla*. When taken with the explanation from the Carthaginian expedition, the 1847 name could mean something like, "cave-dwelling hairy woman."

***Gulo gulo* — wolverine.** The scientific name appears to come from the Latin word "gulosus," meaning "gluttonous," which is in reference to this animal's reputation as an aggressive predator and scavenger. However, this might be an example of folk etymology that resulted from loose and evolving translations of the animal's name over time. The less common name for the animal in Norwegian is "fjellfross," meaning "mountain cat." It is thought that "fjellfross" worked its way into German as the similar-sounding word "vielfrasz," meaning "glutton." The German name then formed the basis for other languages to call the wolverine, "glutton." The English name "wolverine" does not reflect gluttony at all. It is of uncertain origin, but it probably means "little wolf" or "one who behaves like a wolf." The wolverine is the largest land-dwelling species of the weasel family (Mustelidae).

Hoolock hoolock — **western hoolock gibbon.** This species of gibbon can be found in India, Bangladesh, Myanmar, and Thailand. Its scientific name comes from the Burmese native name, "hulluk," and might be imitative of its cry.

Hyaena hyaena — **striped hyena.** The word "hyaena" comes from the Greek word "hus," meaning "pig." This is likely a reference to the animal's mane, which was thought to resemble a hog's bristles. The striped hyena is one of four extant species in the family Hyaenidae, which also includes the tautonymously named spotted hyena (*Crocuta crocuta*). There is debate over whether striped hyena subspecies should be recognized as valid, with some sources stating that the Indian striped hyena is a subspecies classified as *Hyaena hyaena hyaena*.

Indri indri — **indri.** Madagascar's largest living lemur is also known by the common name, babakoto. The name "indri" probably comes from the Malagasy name for the animal, "endrina." The name is often incorrectly attributed to the word "indry," meaning "there it is." As the story goes, the French naturalist who first described the animal in modern taxonomy supposedly heard a Malagasy say "indry" when pointing to the animal. More likely, the naturalist actually heard the Malagasy say, "endrina." The common name "babakoto" is also interesting and is usually translated to mean something like "ancestor." It is a combination of the Malagasy words for "father" and "little boy," roughly meaning "father of the little boy." In terms of subspecies, one source in 2005 listed two subspecies, including *Indri indri indri*, but subsequent research suggests that the two proposed subspecies are not sufficiently different to warrant separate taxons.

Jaculus jaculus — **lesser Egyptian jerboa.** This small rodent can be found in Africa and the Middle East. The scientific name "jaculus" comes from the

Latin word "jaculari," meaning "to throw a javelin." The name is apparently in reference to the fact that this small creature—which is only 5 to 6 inches long—can leap a distance of nearly 7 feet.

Lagurus lagurus — **steppe vole.** This small, plump rodent is similar in appearance to the Norwegian lemming (*Lemmus lemmus*) and is also known as the steppe lemming. The scientific name "lagurus" comes from the Greek words "lagos" and "oura" meaning "hare" and "tail," respectively. The steppe vole has a short tail, similar to that of a hare. Adults have bodies roughly 12 centimeters in length, and tails of only 2 centimeters.

Lemmus lemmus — **Norwegian lemming.** The scientific name is a Latinization of the Norwegian word "lemming," which comes from the Old Norse "lomundr." There are many misconceptions about lemmings, including that they are sometimes driven to mass suicide by jumping off cliffs. This is not a mass suicide but rather a result of migratory behavior in which some lemmings may choose to jump from cliffs into large bodies of water where they may swim in search of new habitats.

Leo leo — **African lion.** The scientific name for this large African cat is the Latin word for "lion." The Latin word was borrowed from the Greek "leon." Many subspecies of this animal were described and named over the 19th and 20th centuries, and many of those subspecies are no longer considered valid. This has resulted in there being many synonyms for this animal, including *Felis leo*, the name given by Carl Linnaeus in 1758. This species no longer has a tautonymous name and is currently classified as *Panthera leo*. Its now-invalid tautonymous name—*Leo leo*—is among the shortest tautonyms.

Lutra lutra — **Eurasian otter.** The origin of this animal's scientific name is unclear, but it might come from the Proto-Indo-European "udreh," coming from the root "wed-," meaning "wet" or "water." The source of the initial "l-" sound may have arisen in connection with "lavo" ("wash"), "lupus" ("wolf," interpreting otters as "water wolves") or "ludo" ("play," referring to the playfulness of otters). The animal is also known as the European otter, the Eurasian river otter, the common otter, and the Old World otter.

Lynx lynx — **Eurasian lynx.** The word "lynx" originated in Middle English and ultimately comes from the Proto-Indo-European root "leuk-" meaning "light" or "brightness" in reference to the luminescence of the animal's reflective eyes, or to its ability to see in the dark, or possibly to its light coloring. This lynx is a medium-sized wild cat native to Europe and Asia, but there are also lynx species native to North America and the Iberian Peninsula. One such species is *Lynx rufus*, also known as the bobcat.

Macrophyllum macrophyllum — **long-legged bat.** The scientific name comes from the Greek words meaning "long leaf," presumably in reference to the bat's long, leaf-shaped nose. The most defining feature of these bats, however, is their long legs that extend farther than most other leaf-nosed bats. At the ends of their legs, they have abnormally large feet equipped with strong claws. They can be found in Central and South America, and they are insectivorous.

Marmota marmota — **alpine marmot.** The alpine marmot is a large, ground-dwelling squirrel found in mountainous areas of central and southern Europe. The origin of the word "marmot" is unclear. It might have come from the Latin phrase "mus montanus," meaning "mountain mouse," which became "murmont" in the Upper Rhine dialect of Romansch.

Martes martes — **pine marten.** Martens, and this pine marten, have bushy tails, large paws, and partially retractable claws. They are mammals within the Mustelidae family, which is one of the largest and most diverse families in the order Carnivora. Other mustelids with tautonymous names include the European badger (*Meles meles*), the wolverine (*Gulo gulo*), and the Eurasian otter (*Lutra lutra*). Skunks were formerly classified as mustelids but are now regarded as a separate family, which includes the striped skunk (*Mephitis mephitis*). The word "martes" is the Latin word for a marten, but the origin of this word prior to its use in Latin is unclear.

Megantereon megantereon — **[no common name].** This prehistoric saber-toothed cat lived in North America, Eurasia, and Africa, and it may have been the ancestor of the well-known saber-toothed tiger (genus *Smilodon*). Its scientific name comes from the Greek words "megas," meaning "large," and "terion," meaning "tool," in reference to the large upper canine teeth that were the primary tools for killing prey. This species no longer has a tautonymous name and is currently classified as *Megantereon cultridens*.

Meles meles — **European badger.** The scientific name is the Latin word for "badger," but it is unclear where this originated. It might have come from the Latin word "feles," for "cat." The common name "badger" is also a bit of a mystery—it may have come from a Middle English or Early Modern English term referring to the "badge-like" white marking on the animal's forehead.

Mephitis mephitis — **striped skunk.** This North American animal's scientific name comes from the Latin word "mephitis," meaning "poisonous gas," which in turn comes from the name of the Samnite goddess Mefitis, who personified the poisonous, foul-smelling gases emitted from swamps and volcanoes. Skunks and all members of the Mephitidae family are noted for their musk-filled scent glands, which they use to deter predators.

Molossus molossus — **velvety free-tailed bat.** This bat was named after the ancient Greek breed of large shepherd dog known as the Molossus, which is believed to be the ancestor of today's mastiff. With its heavily wrinkled face, this bat is reminiscent of a bulldog or mastiff. It occurs in the Americas and is common in the Caribbean.

Monachus monachus — **Mediterranean monk seal.** The scientific name for this seal comes from the Greek word "monakhos," meaning "solitary." This word, in turn, is where the work "monk" comes from. These seals are not always solitary and may live in colonies in certain areas, so the name is more likely in reference to the rings of fat around their necks, which may look like a monk's hood or cowl. They are currently considered endangered, and it is estimated that fewer than 700 individuals live in three or four populations in the Mediterranean Sea.

Mops mops — **Malayan free-tailed bat.** The origin of the name "mops" is unclear. One source states that "mops" comes from a Malay word for "bat," but this is difficult to verify since no current Malay word for "bat" seems to sound anything like "mops." (The word for "bat" in modern Malay is "kelawar.") Another explanation is that the name comes from the German and Dutch word for a pug dog, "mops." This seems plausible given that Malaysia had Dutch colonial presence in the years before this animal was first described. Moreover, the family name, Molossidae, comes from the name of an ancient dog breed, the Molossus. The likening to a pug could come from similarities in the bat's face shape to that of a 19th century pug, which had cropped ears and a longer nose than today's pug.

Myospalax myospalax — **Siberian zokor.** Zokors are burrowing rodents similar to mole-rats. They are native to China, Kazakhstan, and Siberian Russia. They have small eyes, no ears, and powerful front claws used for digging. The word "zokor" appears to be the native name for this animal given by inhabitants of the Altai mountain range in central and eastern Asia. The origin of the scientific name is unclear, but it appears to be a combination of two Latinized Greek words: "muos" meaning "mouse," and "spalax" meaning "mole." This is consistent with the classification of this animal as being closely related to "mole-rats" within the Muroidea ("mouse form") superfamily and the Spalacidae ("mole form") family.

Myotis myotis — **greater mouse-eared bat.** The name "myotis" comes from the Greek words for "mouse ear," referring to the animal's ears, which are quite long for a bat. *Myotis* bats are part of the Vespertilionidae family, which is the most diverse and widely distributed of all bat families. The family takes its name from the Latin word "vesper," meaning "evening." These bats were once referred to as "evening birds" and are found throughout Europe.

Nasua nasua — **South American coati.** This animal is also known as the ring-tailed coati and gets its scientific name from the Latin word "nasus," meaning "nose." This is in reference to the animal's unusual nose, which is quite long, flexible, and almost like an elephant's trunk. The common name "coati" is the native Tupi name for this animal. It has an etymological relationship to, but is not short for, "coatimundi," which means "lone coati." The original scientific name for this animal, proposed by Carl Linnaeus in 1766, was *Viverra nasua*. The animal was later reclassified to the genus *Nasua*, making its name a tautonym.

Niviventer niviventer — **white-bellied rat.** The scientific name comes from the Latin words "nivi," meaning "snow," and "venter," meaning "belly." This rodent and the many others in the *Niviventer* genus are native to southeastern Asia.

Nombe nombe — **[no common name].** This extinct kangaroo from the late Pleistocene epoch was found on the island of New Guinea. It was classified as *Protemnodon nombe* until 2022, when it was reclassified under the new genus, *Nombe*, in light of a new review of the animal's dental attributes. Its scientific name refers to the location of origin of the only known specimens of this animal, which is the Nombe Rockshelter in Papua New Guinea.

Orca orca — **killer whale.** This toothed whale, also known as the orca, is the largest member of the oceanic dolphin family. It is recognizable by its black-and-white patterned body, and it can be found in all the world's oceans. Its scientific name is the Latin word for "whale." An earlier belief that the word is associated with the Latin word "orcus," meaning "underworld," is now understood to be folk etymology. The animal's common name refers to the fact that it is an aggressive predator. This species no longer has a tautonymous name and is currently classified as *Orcinus orca*.

Oreotragus oreotragus — **klipspringer.** The scientific name of this small antelope comes from the Greek words "oros," for "mountain," and "tragos," for "he-goat." Indeed, these sturdy little antelopes can be found in rocky and mountainous terrain in eastern and southern Africa. The common name is a combination of the Afrikaans words "klip," meaning "rock," and "springer," meaning "leaper." Its sure-footedness on rocky terrain is impressive.

Panthera panthera — **leopard.** Whether the leopard, currently classified as *Panthera pardus*, ever had a tautonymous name is unclear. One source states that this large cat of Africa and Asia was once named *Panthera panthera*, but most other sources that provide the naming history of this animal do not identify any tautonyms. Rather, it seems that *Felis pardus* was the first name assigned by Carl Linnaeus in 1758, and that the generic name changed to *Leopardus* and *Panthera* without the specific name ever changing from *pardus*. It would appear that the source that listed the tautonym mistakenly interpreted the abbreviated name "*P. p. panthera*" for the Barbary leopard subspecies as "*Panthera panthera panthera*" instead of the correct name, "*Panthera pardus panthera*." (This subspecies has since been re-classified and is now *Panthera pardus pardus*, which is also not a tautonym.) Both the words "panthera" and "pardus" are Latin words for "panther," with "pardus" referring specifically to males. The word "leopard" comes from the two Latin words "leo" and "pardus."

Papio papio — **Guinea baboon.** This Old World monkey inhabits a small area of western Africa. The origin of the word "papio" is unclear. One source indicates that it comes from the French word, "papion," apparently meaning "baboon." Other sources indicate a connection to the ancient Egyptian baboon god, "Babi." This Egyptian name might also have some etymological relationship to the common name "baboon."

Petaurista petaurista — **red giant flying squirrel.** The scientific name for this nocturnal rodent comes from the Greek word "petauron" for "perch" or "springboard," and the Latin suffix "-ista" denoting ability. The name therefore means something like "springboard jumper." Like other flying squirrels, this animal has the ability to glide long distances between trees and cannot actually fly like a bird or bat. This species is one of the largest flying squirrels.

Phocoena phocoena — **harbor porpoise.** The common name "porpoise" comes from Medieval Latin "porcopiscus," which is a combination of words for "pig" and "fish." The scientific name is a Latinized form of the Greek word "phokaina," meaning "big seal." The harbor porpoise is widespread in cooler coastal waters of the northern Atlantic, northern Pacific, and the Black Sea. One of the first people to distinguish whales, dolphins, and porpoises from fish was Aristotle in his *Historia Animalium*, which is where the Greek reference to "big seal" first appears. Synonyms for this animal's scientific name include the tautonymous names *Phocaena phocaena* and *Phocena phocena*.

Pipistrellus pipistrellus — **common pipistrelle.** With a Palearctic distribution, this microbat can be found across a large range including most of Europe, northern Africa, and southern Asia. According to most sources, its scientific name comes from the word "pipistrello," meaning "bat" in Italian. "Vespertilio," the Latin word for "bat" that comes from a Latin word meaning "evening," was assimilated into the similar sounding word "pipistrello." Echolocation calls of this species were studied in 1999 and differences in the frequency of the calls resulted in this species being subdivided into the common pipistrelle and the soprano pipistrelle. Reclassification of the common pipistrelle has occurred many times since it was originally described and placed in the genus *Vespertilio* in 1774. Later, in 1839, it was reclassified to the genus *Vesperugo*. Yet again, in 1897, it was reclassified to its own genus *Pipistrellus*, creating the tautonym. Just as the term microbat suggests, this species is small at less than 3.4 inches long from the top of its head to the tip of its tail. Subspecies once included *Pipistrellus pipistrellus pipistrellus* and *Pipistrellus pipistrellus aladdin*, but the latter is now considered a separate species.

Pithecia pithecia — **white-faced saki.** The scientific name of this New World monkey comes from the Greek word "pithekos" for "monkey." The common name "saki" is derived from a Tupi word for this animal. Other common names for this species include the Guianan saki and the golden-faced saki. Its subspecies include *Pithecia pithecia pithecia*, although this genus has undergone taxonomic revision in recent years and this subspecies may no longer be considered valid.

***Putorius putorius* — European polecat.** This mustelid native to eastern Eurasia and northern Africa is also known as the common polecat and the forest polecat. It has a more compact body than other mustelids and is known for its ability to secrete foul-smelling liquids to mark its territory. The origin of the common name "polecat" is unclear, and likely derives from the French word "poule," meaning "chicken," in reference to the animal's fondness for poultry, or alternatively comes from the Old English "ful," meaning "foul." Its scientific name comes from the Latin word "putor," meaning "a bad smell." This species no longer has a tautonymous name and is currently classified as *Mustela putorius*.

***Rattus rattus* — black rat.** This rodent has many common names, like ship rat and house rat. The origin of its scientific name is unclear but could come from the Proto-Germanic "rattaz" or the Latin "rattus." It might instead have originated from Middle Persian "randitan," or from Sanskrit "radati." All of these seem to refer to rats in some sense, but it is unclear which came first or whether they were developed independently. One challenge in determining the origin of this name is the fact that it is hard to tell where on the globe rats originated, and when they spread from region to region. It is thought that the original word—whatever it was—meant "to gnaw, scrape, or bite." Three subspecies were once recognized, including *Rattus rattus rattus*, but today they are considered invalid as merely color morphs.

***Redunca redunca* — bohor reedbuck.** This antelope is native to central Africa. Its scientific name is Latin for "bent backwards" or "curved," in reference to the animal's horns, which come out at a backwards direction from its head.

***Rupicapra rupicapra* — chamois.** This species of goat-antelope is native to mountains in Europe. Its scientific name comes from the Latin words "rupes," meaning "rock," and "capra," meaning "female goat." The common name "chamois" appears to have come from a 16th century French word, but its ultimate origin is unknown. Chamois are hunted by lynxes, leopards, wolves, bears, eagles, and humans. They use speed to escape predators and can run at 31 miles per hour. They can also jump 6.6 feet vertically into the air or over a distance of 20 feet.

Saccolaimus saccolaimus — **naked-rumped pouched bat.** The name of this bat comes from the Greek words "sakkos" for a "sack or bag," and "laimos" for "a throat." This bat has a small sack on its throat, the purpose of which has not been fully understood. This bat is unusual in that it has white fur. It is also known as the pouched tomb bat and can be found in southeastern Asia.

Strepsiceros strepsiceros — **greater kudu.** This woodland antelope is found throughout eastern and southern Africa. The common name "kudu" is the Khoekhoe name for this antelope. Its scientific name comes from the Greek words "strepsis" for "twisting," and "keras" for "horn," in reference to the long, twisting horns of this animal. This species no longer has a tautonymous name and is currently classified as *Tragelaphus strepsiceros*.

Uncia uncia — **snow leopard.** This felid, also known as the ounce, is native to the mountains of central and southern Asia. Its global population is estimated as fewer than 10,000 mature individuals, and because this number is expected to decline significantly in the coming years, it is considered vulnerable to extinction. The snow leopard was long classified in its own genus, *Uncia*, but genetic testing has revealed that it belongs in the same genus as the lion, tiger, jaguar, and leopard. As a result, this species no longer has a tautonymous name and is currently classified as *Panthera uncia*. The history of the scientific name is an unusual one and appears to involve false splitting of an earlier name for another tautonymous felid. The ancient Greeks were familiar with a moderate-sized feline and called it "lynx." The Romans borrowed the Greek word, which then became "lonza." This word passed into Old French and become "lonce." The word "lonce" was incorrectly interpreted as "l'once," in which the initial consonant "l" was mistaken for the definite article "la," meaning "the." As a result, the name of the animal was perceived as simply "once." The word "once" passed into Spanish as "onca" and English as "ounce," and was eventually Latinized to "uncia." The word "uncia" was assigned to the snow leopard when it was described as *Felis uncia* in 1777.

Vicugna vicugna — **vicuna.** The word "vicugna" is the Peruvian name for this animal, which lives in the Andes Mountains in Peru, Bolivia, Chile, and Argentina. Vicunas produce small amounts of extremely fine wool, which is very expensive because the animal can only be shorn every three years and has to be caught from the wild. This animal was reclassified to the *Lama* genus in 2021 by the American Society of Mammalogists, giving the animal a new scientific name of *Lama vicugna*.

Vulpes vulpes — **red fox.** The red fox is the largest of the true foxes and one of the most widely distributed carnivorans. It is found across parts of northern Africa and the entire Northern Hemisphere. Its common name comes from a Proto-Indo-European word meaning "thick-haired" or "tail" that eventually became "fox" in Old English. Its scientific name is the word for this animal in Latin. It is thought that the original name for the fox is lost to history, having been considered a "taboo word" by ancient people who held beliefs rooted in superstition. The ancient fear was that by saying the name of dangerous animals aloud, they would somehow invite those animals into their community, which could have unwanted consequences including animal attacks on people or livestock, for example. So instead of calling the dangerous animal by its actual name, ancient people substituted the name with a harmless synonym—like "the one with the bushy tail"—that was believed to be a safer way of referring to the animal.

PART III:

BIRDS

Nycticorax nycticorax

BIRDS ARE WARM-BLOODED VERTEBRATES GENERALLY characterized by feathers, toothless beaked jaws, the laying of hard-shelled eggs, four-chambered hearts, and strong but lightweight skeletons. The diversity of bird species on the planet and on this list is impressive. Using this list of birds alone,

one can encounter many different ecosystems, peoples, and languages. Of note, more than half of all bird species and many on this list are passerine birds of the order Passeriformes (from Latin meaning "sparrow-shaped").

Ajaja ajaja— **roseate spoonbill.** This wading bird of the ibis and spoonbill family is found in North and South America. Its pink color is caused by its diet, like that of the American flamingo. Its scientific name comes from a native Tupi word for this spoonbill. This species no longer has a tautonymous name and is currently classified as *Platalea ajaja*.

Alle alle — **little auk.** The little auk is a bird found in marine cliffsides around the Atlantic Ocean and the Norwegian Sea. The word "auk" is derived from the Proto-Germanic word, "alko," meaning "sea bird." The name "alle" is the Sami word for the long-tailed duck, which is onomatopoeic of the drake duck's call. It appears that Carl Linnaeus was not familiar with the winter plumages of these birds and confused the auk with the long-tailed duck when naming it.

Amandava amandava — **red avadavat.** This small, red bird is popular as a pet. Its scientific and common names are corruptions of the Indian city name Ahmedabad, which is where the first few specimens of these birds were obtained for study by European taxonomists.

Amazilia amazilia — **amazilia hummingbird.** This hummingbird has a distinctive, black-tipped red bill and red feathers. It also has a turquoise-green throat and a bronze-green belly. The scientific name likely comes from a Spanish-American word and has some connection to the Amazon River. This species occurs in western Peru and southwestern Ecuador. This species no longer has a tautonymous name and is currently classified as *Amazilis amazilia*.

Anhinga anhinga — **anhinga.** There are a few different explanations for how this large New World bird, sometimes called the snakebird, darter, or water turkey, got its scientific name. One states that the word "anhinga" is the Tupi language name for the animal, which means "water turkey." Another explanation states that the name comes from the Latin "anguinus," meaning "snaky," in reference to the fact that when the bird swims, only the neck appears above water, so the bird looks like a snake ready to strike. A third explanation states that the Tupi language name for the bird translates to "snake bird" or "devil bird." A fourth explanation states that the Tupi language name means "small head." Like other darters, the anhinga hunts by spearing fish using its sharp, slender beak.

Anser anser — **graylag goose.** This large goose gets its scientific name from the Latin word for "goose." The greylag goose was one of the first animals to be domesticated, which happened at least 3,000 years ago in Ancient Egypt. The domestic subspecies is known as *Anser anser domesticus.* This species has a Palearctic distribution.

Antigone antigone — **sarus crane.** This large, nonmigratory crane is found in India, southeastern Asia, and Australia. It is the tallest of the flying birds, standing almost 6 feet tall. The scientific name is based on Greek mythology. Antigone of Troy was the daughter of the Trojan king Laomedon. She was turned into a stork for comparing her own beauty with that of the goddess Hera. Carl Linnaeus appears to have confused this myth with that of Gerana, queen of the pigmies, who considered herself more beautiful than Hera and was turned into a crane (not a stork). Both stories can be found in Ovid's *Metamorphoses.* This species of crane was previously placed in the genus *Grus,* but a study published in 2010 resulted in this crane being reassigned to the genus *Antigone,* creating a tautonym. The common name "sarus" comes from the Hindi name "saras" for the species, which comes from the Sanskrit word "sarasa" for "lake bird." Native Australians call this species "the crane that dips its head in blood."

Apus apus — **common swift.** The scientific name of this medium-sized Old World bird comes from Greek and means "without foot," referring to the fact that swifts have very short legs that are sometimes hard to see and rarely used for walking on the ground. Swifts use their small legs primarily for clinging to vertical surfaces, which is why their common name in German is "mauersegler," literally meaning "wall-glider."

***Bonasia bonasia* — hazel grouse.** This small grouse has a Palearctic distribution and is found in dense coniferous woodlands. It is also known as the hazel hen in light of its brown wings and chestnut-colored underparts. The origin of its scientific name is unclear and there are numerous potential explanations. One explanation states that the word comes from the Greek word "bonasos" for "bull," apparently in reference to the fact that males of this bird make a sound similar to that of a bull. Another explanation is that the word comes from the Latin words "bonum" and "assum" meaning "good roast," referring to the bird as a food source. Yet another explanation links the name to the bird's shy behavior, stating that the Greek word "bonasos" refers specifically to bulls whose horns were unfit for fighting and were therefore shy. This species no longer has a tautonymous name and is currently classified as *Tetrastes bonasia*.

***Bubo bubo* — Eurasian eagle-owl.** Many habitats throughout Eurasia are home to this large, impressive species of owl, including mountainous regions and other rocky areas. Additionally, they can be found in coniferous forests and other woodlands at varied elevations. Relatively remote habitats are preferred, although they have also been found in farmlands and parks within European cities. German speakers often call this bird by the common name "uhu," which is imitative of its deep, far-carrying song. One of the largest species of owl, females can grow to a total length of 30 inches and a wingspan of 6 feet, 2 inches. The scientific name of this bird is a Latin word referring to this specific type of owl, but it is unclear where the word came from or why it was used in this way. Similar to the common buzzard (*Buteo buteo*), this bird's name might have some etymological relationship with the Latin word "bubo" meaning "I cry like a bittern," in reference to its terrifying, extremely loud hooting cry. Subspecies include *Bubo bubo bubo*, which is the darkest and most richly colored of the eagle-owl subspecies and has the distinctive orange eyes and ear tufts characteristic of the species.

Buteo buteo — **common buzzard.** This bird of prey's name comes from the Latin word "buteo" for a hawk or falcon, but the origin of the Latin word is unclear. One source—often repeated—states that the word "buteo" is onomatopoeic of the bird's call. This is questionable since none of the calls of this bird seem to sound anything like "buteo," and are usually more like the "kee-yarrr" scream common among hawks. Another possibility is that "buteo" is derivative of "butio," the Latin word for a bittern, which is a marsh bird that makes a deep, booming call during mating season. Perhaps the ancient Romans thought that the buzzard's cry was startling and ominous, like the bittern's, and so referred to the buzzard with a nearly identical word. It is also plausible that the Latin "butio" bears some etymological relationship to "bubo," which is the Latin word for both, "I cry like a bittern," and the tautonymously named Eurasian eagle-owl, *Bubo bubo.* The word "buzzard" is also a source of some confusion as in North America it refers colloquially to the turkey vulture, which is not a hawk or a member of the *Buteo* genus.

Calliope calliope — **Siberian rubythroat.** This migratory insectivorous species lives in coniferous forests in Siberia. Its scientific name comes from the Greek word meaning "beautiful-voiced." The Greek mythological muse Calliope presided over eloquence and epic poetry. This bird's common name refers to the patch of bright red feathers on its throat, which stands out in vivid color against the bird's mostly brown plumage.

Cardinalis cardinalis — **northern cardinal.** This bird is also known as the common cardinal or red cardinal. It can be found in southeastern Canada, through the eastern United States from Maine to Minnesota to Texas, and south through Mexico, Belize, and Guatemala. The name refers to the cardinals of the Roman Catholic Church, who wear distinctive red robes and caps. Note that only male cardinals have the vibrant red coloring. Females are more olive colored. The northern cardinal was one of the original animals classified by Carl Linnaeus in 1758, and the subspecies he described is now classified as *Cardinalis cardinalis cardinalis.*

Carduelis carduelis — **European goldfinch.** The scientific name is the Latin word for "goldfinch." The name "carduelis" originally comes from the Latin word "carduus," meaning "thistle," in reference to the seeding thistle heads that this bird eats. The bird is native to Europe, northern Africa, and western and central Asia.

Casuarius casuarius — **southern cassowary.** This large, flightless bird can be found in Indonesia, Papua New Guinea, and northeastern Australia. The scientific name is derived from its Malay name "kesuari" for this family of birds.

Chloris chloris — **European greenfinch.** The scientific name for this small, green bird comes from the Greek word "khloris," which is the Greek name for the bird, from "khloros," meaning "green." The bird is widespread throughout Europe, northern Africa, and southwestern Asia.

Chlorura chlorura — **green-tailed towhee.** This colorful member of the American sparrow family can be recognized by the bright green stripes on the edge of its wings, a white throat, and a red cap on its head. Its breeding range covers the western United States, and its winter range includes Mexico and the southwestern United States. Its scientific name comes from the Greek words "khloros" for "green," and "oura" for "tail," in reference to its green tail. This species no longer has a tautonymous name and is currently classified as *Pipilo chlorurus*.

Ciconia ciconia — **white stork.** This large Old World bird in the stork family has black and white plumage, and long red legs. The scientific name is the Latin word for "stork," as originally recorded in the works of Horace and Ovid. The word "stork" comes from the Old English "storc."

Cinclus cinclus — **white-throated dipper.** This bird, found in Europe, the Middle East, central Asia, and India, is also known as the European dipper. It gets its scientific name from the Greek word "kinklos," which refers to small, tail-wagging birds that live near water. The common name "dipper" is descriptive of their ability to obtain food by diving underwater, which they can do without the help of webbed feet.

Clanga clanga — **greater spotted eagle.** This large bird of prey is distributed across Europe and Asia. The origin of its scientific name is unclear. One explanation is that the name comes from the Greek word for "scream," possibly in reference to the bird's call. However, according to other interpretations, the name is from the Greek word "klangos," an alternate form of "plangos," for "a kind of eagle" mentioned by Aristotle.

Coccothraustes coccothraustes — **hawfinch.** The scientific name of this European finch is derived from the Greek "kokkos" meaning "seed," and "thrauo" meaning "to break" or "to shatter." This bird's food is mainly seeds and fruit kernels, especially those of cherries, which it cracks with its powerful bill. The common name "hawfinch" refers to the red berries of the common hawthorn.

Cochlearius cochlearius — **boat-billed heron.** The scientific name of this unusual-looking bird comes from the Latin word "cochlearium," meaning "spoon," in reference to the bird's broad, scoop-like bill. The word "cochlearium" itself comes from the word "cochlea," meaning "snail shell," leading many to conclude that ancient Romans used small spoons with long handles to eat snails out of their shells. This bird is nocturnal and lives in mangrove swamps from Mexico south to Peru and Brazil where it feeds on a variety of small mammals, amphibians, insects, small fish, and mollusks.

Colius colius — **white-backed mousebird.** This bird from southern Africa gets its scientific name from the Greek word "kolios," apparently meaning "green woodpecker." It is not clear why this white-backed mousebird, which is not green, was given this name. The common name "mousebird" refers to this bird's habit of creeping along branches of trees with its body horizontal and close to the branch, like a mouse.

Coscoroba coscoroba — **coscoroba swan.** This large waterfowl is native to southern South America. Although its wingspan can exceed 5 feet, it is considered small for a swan. The scientific name likely comes from "cosaroba," a Tupi name for a swan-like diving bird.

Coturnix coturnix — **common quail.** The scientific name of this bird is the Latin name for the common quail. The common name "quail" is a bit of a mystery. It may have come from Medieval Latin "quaccula," or a similar word in a Germanic language, perhaps imitative of the bird's call.

Coeligena coeligena — **bronzy inca.** The scientific name appears to be a Latin word meaning "heaven-born" or "celestial," but it is not clear why this genus of South American hummingbird has this name. The word "inca" comes from a Spanish word meaning "king."

Cotinga cotinga — **purple-breasted cotinga.** The name "cotinga" comes from the Tupi language. One source states that the Tupi word means "bright forest bird." Another source states that it comes from the Tupi words "coting," meaning "to wash," and "tinga," meaning "white," although the reason for this name is unclear. The purple-breasted cotinga is found in Brazil, Colombia, French Guiana, Guyana, Peru, Suriname, and Venezuela. It lives in topical lowland forests. True to its name, males have vivid purple feathers on their breasts. They also have bright blue heads, backs, and undersides.

Crex crex — **corn crake.** The scientific name of this medium-sized, Eurasian, ground-living bird is onomatopoeic of this bird's call, which is a loud "krek krek." This loud call can be heard from almost one mile away and serves to establish the breeding territory and attract females.

Crossoptilon crossoptilon — **white eared pheasant.** This Asian bird get its common name from its white coloration and its prominent ear tufts—not because it has white ears. It is more of a "white, eared" pheasant rather than a "white-eared" (hyphenated) pheasant. The indigenous people of Himalaya call it "shagga," meaning "snow fowl." The scientific name comes from the Greek words "krossoi," meaning "fringe," and "ptilon," meaning "feathers," in reference to the two ear-like tufts of feathers on its head.

Curaeus curaeus — **austral blackbird.** This small, dark bird can be found in forests in Argentina and Chile. The scientific name appears to come from the word "kuri," meaning "black," in the Mapuzugun language of the Mapuche people in south-central Chile and west-central Argentina. The feathers of this bird are completely glossy black.

Curruca curruca — **lesser whitethroat.** This warbler can be found in temperate Europe and in the western and central Palearctic. It winters in sub-Saharan Africa, Arabia, and India. Its scientific name is the Latin word for an unidentified small bird mentioned by the Roman poet Juvenal.

Cyanicterus cyanicterus — **blue-backed tanager.** The word "cyanicterus" is formed from the Greek "kuanos," meaning "dark-blue," and "ikteros," meaning "jaundice-yellow." This name refers to the bird's bright blue and yellow feathers. This species is the only member of the genus *Cyanicterus* and there are no recognized subspecies. It is found in a relatively small area at the borders of Brazil, French Guiana, Guyana, Suriname, and Venezuela.

Cygnus cygnus —**common swan.** This bird's scientific name is the Latin word for "swan." It is also known as the whooper swan because of its "whooping" call. It is a large swan found throughout Eurasia. Young swans are called "cygnets."

Diuca diuca — **common diuca finch.** The scientific name of this southern South American tanager comes from the Mapuche name for this species, "diuca" or "siuca." It is the only species in the *Diuca* genus, although there are four subspecies, including *Diuca diuca diuca.*

Dives dives — **melodious blackbird.** This tropical bird from Central America has a scientific name that is difficult to trace. It appears to come from the Latin word for "wealthy" or "costly," but it is unclear why the bird would be given this name. One source suggests that the name refers to the shiny appearance of the bird's plumage, as well as its proud look.

Domicella domicella — **purple-naped lory.** This colorful parrot of Indonesia is mostly red with green wings and blue thighs. Its scientific name is the Medieval Latin word for "young lady" or "damsel." It is currently considered endangered and is threatened by excessive trapping for the cage-bird trade. This species no longer has a tautonymous name and is currently classified as *Lorius domicella*.

Ensifera ensifera — **sword-billed hummingbird.** This hummingbird from the Andean regions of South America gets its scientific name from the Latin words "ensis," meaning "sword," and "ferre," meaning "to wield or carry," in reference to this bird's remarkable beak length. It is the only bird to have a beak longer than the rest of its body, which it uses to drink nectar from flowers with long corollas. This hummingbird has coevolved with the plant species *Passiflora mixta*, a perennial vine identified by large pink flowers. While most hummingbirds preen using their bills, this species must use its feet to scratch and preen due to its bill being so long.

Erythrogenys erythrogenys — **rusty-cheeked scimitar babbler.** This bird, found in southeastern Asia, gets its scientific name from the Greek words "erythros," meaning "red," and "genys," meaning "cheek," in reference to the reddish coloring on its face. The scimitar babblers are among the so-called "Old World babblers," which is something of a taxonomic dumping ground. During much of the 20th century, the Old World babbler family (Timaliidae) was used as a "wastebin taxon," meaning a catch-all taxon that has the sole purpose of classifying organisms that do not fit anywhere else. Numerous hard-to-place songbirds were put into this family. German ornithologist Ernst Hartert jokingly said in 1910, "What one can't place systematically is considered an Old World babbler." However, in recent years and with the aid of DNA sequence data, taxonomists have been able to organize and reclassify most of the Old World babblers. The family current includes 56 species divided into ten genera.

Falcipennis falcipennis — **Siberian grouse.** This short, rotund, forest-dwelling grouse gets its name from Latin words meaning "sickle-winged," in reference to the bird's wings, which have long, sharp-looking primary feathers. Primary feathers are the "fingertip" feathers and the farthest from the bird's body when the wings are extended. The shape of the primaries is thought to help the bird make sharp turns in flight—a helpful tool when escaping danger in dense forests—and to make unique "flight sounds" to communicate with other Siberian grouses.

Francolinus francolinus — **black francolin.** The scientific name of this pheasant found in the Middle East and the Indian subcontinent comes from Old Italian for "little hen" or "partridge." One source suggests that the name ultimately comes from a word meaning "free fowl" as common people were forbidden from taking them because Italian royalty had granted them the freedom of living.

Galbula galbula — **green-tailed jacamar.** This small, South American bird gets its scientific name from the Latin word meaning "small yellow bird," ultimately from the Latin word "galbus" for "yellow." This bird is only 7 to 8.7 inches long and weighs less than one ounce.

Gallinago gallinago — **common snipe.** This small, stocky, Old World bird wades in mud and shallow water to forage for food and is therefore known as a "wader." Its scientific name comes from the Latin words "gallina," for "hen," and the suffix "-ago," for "resembling."

Gallus gallus — **red junglefowl.** This tropical bird ranges across much of southeastern Asia and parts of southern Asia. Its scientific name comes from the Latin word for "cock." The red junglefowl is the ancestor of the domesticated chicken (*Gallus gallus domesticus*), which was created roughly 8,000 years ago. Numerous other subspecies exist, including *Gallus gallus gallus*.

Granatina granatina — **violet-eared waxbill.** This bird is also known as the common grenadier and can be found in drier areas of southern Africa. It has vivid purple, red, blue, orange, and grey coloring. The origin of its scientific name is unclear. One source indicates that it came from the French name "le grenadin" and the Latin word "granatinus," meaning "grenadier" in English. However, "granatina" might instead have come from French or Italian words for "pomegranate," or from the Latin "granatum" for "seeded," possibly in reference to the bird's diet.

Grus grus — **common crane.** This medium-sized crane is the only crane found in Europe and is also known as the Eurasian crane. The scientific name "grus" is the Latin word for "crane." The origin of the word "crane" is unclear, but it might come from the sound of the bird's cry, as interpreted by ancient humans.

Guarouba guarouba — **golden parakeet.** This medium-sized golden-yellow parrot is native to the Amazon Basin of interior northern Brazil. It lives in drier, upland rainforests, and it is threatened by deforestation and flooding, as well as by the illegal trading of these parrots as pets. Its scientific name comes from the Tupi word "guarajuba," meaning "yellow bird." This species no longer has a tautonymous name and is currently classified as *Guaruba guarouba*. The tautonymous name appears to have resulted from a misspelling.

Guira guira — **guira cuckoo.** This South American bird gets its scientific name from the Guarani word "guira," meaning "bird." The Guarani language is a South American language that belongs to the Tupian family of languages and is commonly used among Paraguayan people today. The word "cuckoo" is onomatopoeic of the bird's call. Unlike many Old Word cuckoos, the guira cuckoo does not practice parasitism by, for instance, placing its eggs in the nest of a different bird.

Himantopus himantopus — **black-winged stilt.** This widely distributed and long-legged wader gets its scientific name from the Greek words "himas," meaning "leather thong," and "pous," meaning "foot." The Greek name "strap foot" or "thong foot," and the common name "stilt," are in reference to the long, thin legs of this bird.

Histrionicus histrionicus — **harlequin duck.** The harlequin duck gets its common name from the Harlequin, a character in popular Italian comedic theatre introduced in the late 16th century. The Harlequin character was identified by his colorful, checkered costume. Likewise, breeding males of this duck boast colorful and complex plumage patterns. The scientific name comes from the Latin word "histrio," meaning "actor," also in reference to the bird's theatrical and harlequin-like appearance. Other common names for this animal include painted duck, totem pole duck, and glacier duck.

Ibis ibis — **yellow-billed stork.** This large African wading stork has white feathers, a red face, and a yellow bill. It is not actually an ibis, despite its scientific name, but a stork. It is widespread in regions south of the Sahara. Its scientific name refers to the similar looking "ibis" birds, which term comes from Latin and Greek for that group of birds. This species no longer has a tautonymous name and is currently classified as *Mycteria ibis*.

Ichthyaetus ichthyaetus — **Pallas's gull.** This large bird, also known as the great black-headed gull, gets its scientific name from the Greek words "ichthys" for "fish," and "aetos" for "eagle." These are exceptionally large gulls—the third largest species of gull in the world—and they do eat fish as the name suggests. This bird is usually found in eastern Europe, the Middle East, India, and other parts of Asia.

Icterus icterus — **Venezuelan troupial.** This national bird of Venezuela is orange, black, and white, and gets its scientific name from the Greek word "ikteros," meaning "jaundice." It was once believed that by looking at this bird—or perhaps a different "icterus" bird—a person would be cured of jaundice and the bird would die. The common name "troupial" comes from the French word "troupiale," meaning "troop," because this bird lives in flocks. The *Icterus* birds are also known as the American orioles, which are distinct from the Old World orioles in the genus *Oriolus*.

Incana incana — **Socotra warbler.** This bird is endemic to Socotra, the largest of the four islands in the Socotra archipelago off the tip of the horn of Africa in the Guardafui Channel. The scientific name comes from the Latin word "incanus," meaning "whitish grey," in reference to the color of the bird's plumage.

Indicator indicator — **greater honeyguide.** This bird is found in Africa and is known for guiding people and animals to nests of wild bees. The greater honeyguide attracts a person's attention by continually calling, then moving on closer to the bees' nest until the person follows. In other situations, it spreads its tail and moves around on its perch to attract a person's attention. Many sources state that this species also guides honey badgers to bees' nests. For many years, naturalists dismissed these stories as tall tales, but it is now accepted that this species does, in fact, guide humans to bees' nests. This bird feeds on the contents of bee colonies, including bee eggs, larvae, pupae, waxworms, and beeswax. Honeyguides are among the few birds that can digest wax. When a human or honey badger opens the nest, the greater honeyguide will join in eating the contents. The greater honeyguide will also enter bees' nests when the bees are sluggish in the early morning and will feed at abandoned nests. The scientific name comes from the Latin word "indicare," meaning "to point out," in reference to the bird guiding humans to bees' nests.

Jacana jacana — **wattled jacana.** This colorful South American wader gets its scientific name from the Portuguese name for this bird, which in turn comes from the Tupi name for the bird, "naha'na." The Tupi name means "alert" or "loud" bird. There are six subspecies, with *Jacana jacana jacana* being the most widespread.

Lagopus lagopus — **willow ptarmigan.** The scientific name for this large, ground-dwelling grouse comes from the Greek words "lagos," for "hare," and "pous," for "foot." It is called a "hare-foot" because of its lower legs and feet, which in winter are covered with feathers like a wooly boot. These feathers help the bird to negotiate frozen ground. The willow ptarmigan is widely distributed in the Northern Hemisphere and nineteen subspecies have been recognized, including *Lagopus lagopus lagopus*. The taxonomy of these subspecies is complicated by the fact that the bird's plumage changes several times a year, making taxonomic analysis sometimes challenging.

Lerwa lerwa — **snow partridge.** This pheasant is widely distributed across the high-altitude Himalayan regions of India, Pakistan, Nepal, and China. The scientific name is a Latinized form of the Nepali word "larwa," meaning "snow partridge." This word resembles and may have come from the Sanskrit "latva," for a bird.

Leucogeranus leucogeranus — **Siberian crane.** This bird, also known as the snow crane, is distinctive among cranes as being nearly completely white, except for its black primary feathers that are visible in flight. Among cranes, they make the longest distance migrations, with populations migrating from the Arctic tundra of Russia in the summer to China in the east and Iran in the west. The scientific name comes from the Greek word "leukos," meaning "white," and "geranos," meaning "crane," in reference to the bird's plumage.

Limosa limosa — **black-tailed godwit.** This long-legged, Old World wader's scientific name is derived from Latin and means "muddy," likely in reference to the bird's habitat of muddy estuaries, swamps, and bogs. The English name "godwit" was first recorded in about 1416 and is believed to imitate the bird's call.

Luscinia luscinia — **thrush nightingale.** The scientific name of this small passerine bird is the Latin word for "nightingale." The word "nightingale" comes from the English word "night" and the Old English word "galan," meaning "to sing." It is a migratory insectivorous species breeding in Europe and wintering in Africa.

Manacus manacus — **white-bearded manakin.** This small South American bird gets its scientific name from the Dutch word "manneken," meaning "small man." This species is rather small, reaching only 4.2 inches long.

Mascarinus mascarinus — **Mascarene parrot.** This extinct parrot was endemic to the Mascarene island of Reunion in the western Indian Ocean. It had a large, red bill and long, rounded tail feathers. It had red legs, a black mask, and partially white tail feathers. Its coloration while it was alive is unclear as there are conflicting reports of what it looked like and only two stuffed specimens exist today. The bird likely had a grey head and a brownish body, but this might be an inaccurate assumption as stuffed specimens may have changed color because of aging and exposure to light. The date and cause of its extinction are unclear. Its scientific name refers to the Mascarene Islands, which were themselves named after their Portuguese discoverer, Pedro Mascarenhas. Whether the valid name of this species is a tautonym is also unclear. This species was originally described by Carl Linnaeus as *Psittacus mascarin* in 1771, with "mascarin" being an abbreviation for "mascarinus." In 1831, some naturalists believed that the bird was found on Madagascar, causing some to name the bird *Mascarinus madagascariensis*. The following year, a German herpetologist reclassified the bird as *Coracopsis mascarina*. Then in 1879, an English zoologist reclassified it as *Mascarinus duboisi*. During much of this time, other dark-colored parrots were described as new species but were sometimes believed by other naturalists to be the same species as the Mascarene parrot. This caused the parrot to get a variety of now-invalid combinations of scientific names, including *Mascarinus obscurus* and *Coracopsis obscura*. In 1891, the bird was reclassified using the 1831 generic name and the 1771 specific name: *Mascarinus mascarinus*. Today, the name *Mascarinus mascarin* is used by the International Ornithological Congress. The International Commission on Zoological Nomenclature has adopted the tautonymous name *Mascarinus mascarinus*.

Melanodera melanodera — **white-bridled finch.** This bird, also known as the canary-winged finch and black-throated finch, is found in grasslands in southern South America. The scientific name comes from the Greek words "melanos," meaning "black," and "dera," meaning "neck" or "throat." As the name suggests, males of this small bird have black throats and masks, which are bordered with white.

Milvus milvus — **red kite.** This medium-large European bird of prey gets its scientific name from the Latin word for "kite" (referring to the bird). The word might have originated from a Proto-Indo-European word meaning "stain," potentially in reference to the coloring on the bird's wings.

Mitu mitu — **Alagoas curassow.** This large, pheasant-like bird is currently extinct in the wild. It was formerly native to forests in northeastern Brazil, in what is now the states of Alagoas and Pernambuco (hence its common name). The bird was first described by a German naturalist in 1648, and even at that time there were so few individuals in existence that the legitimacy of the species was questioned due to lack of specimens. The bird was rediscovered in 1951, and it was determined that fewer than 60 individuals remained in the wild. Despite efforts to preserve this bird's habitat, its forests were destroyed for sugarcane agriculture. The scientific name comes from the Tupi name for this bird, which means "black skinned." It is a beautiful bird—its feathers are black and glossy with a blue-purple hue, its beak is bright red with a white tip, and its legs and feet are red.

Nycticorax nycticorax — **black-crowned night heron.** This medium-sized heron is found throughout most of the world, except for the coldest regions and Australasia. Adults have black feathers on the tops of their heads and backs, with white or pale grey bodies, red eyes, and yellow legs. Their bodies are unusually shaped for herons—they are stocky with shorter bills, legs, and necks, making their resting posture appear somewhat hunched. The scientific name means "night raven," and comes from the Greek words "nuktos," meaning "night," and "korax," meaning "raven." This name refers to the largely nocturnal feeding habits and crow-like call of this species.

Nyctea nyctea — **snowy owl.** This large, white owl is also known as the polar owl, the white owl, and the Arctic owl. It is native to the Arctic regions of North America and the Palearctic. Its scientific name comes from the Greek word "nuktos," meaning "night," but this is a misleading name because the owl is very active during the daytime when it hunts lemmings and other small mammals. This is unusual behavior for owls, which usually hunt at night.

This species no longer has a tautonymous name and is currently classified as *Bubo scandiacus*.

***Oenanthe oenanthe* — northern wheatear.** This small bird can be found in Europe, and in northern and central Asia. It has one of the longest migration journeys of any small bird, flying from sub-Saharan Africa in spring over a large portion of the Northern Hemisphere. Its scientific name comes from the Greek words "oine," meaning "wine" or "vine," and "anthos," meaning "flower." This name refers to the bird's appearance in Greece after migrating in the spring when grapevines blossom.

***Oriolus oriolus* — Eurasian golden oriole.** The common name "oriole" is an adaptation of the scientific name, which comes from the Latin word "aureoles," meaning "golden." As the name suggests, this bird has vivid yellow plumage. The *Oriolus* orioles of the Old Word are not closely related to the New World orioles of the genus *Icterus*.

***Pampa pampa* — wedge-tailed sabrewing.** This hummingbird is found in lowland tropical forests and degraded former forests of Belize, Guatemala, Honduras, and Mexico. Its scientific name appears to come from the Spanish word for "plain" or "prairie" due to the mistaken belief that this bird came from the interior plains of La Plata, Argentina.

***Pauxi pauxi* — helmeted curassow.** This large terrestrial bird is mostly black with a red bill and a distinctive grey casque on its forehead. The bird is currently endangered and lives in the eastern Andes of Venezuela and Colombia. The scientific name comes from the Spanish word "pauji" for "peacock." This word was used for a variety of large gamebirds by early settlers in tropical South America.

***Perdix perdix* — grey partridge.** This bird, also known as the English partridge, the Hungarian partridge, and the hun, is a pheasant that is widespread through much of Europe, Asia, and (through introduction) North America. The scientific name is the Latin word for "partridge."

Petronia petronia — **rock sparrow.** This small sparrow breeds on barren rocky hills from the Iberian Peninsula and northwestern Africa across southern Europe to Asia. Its scientific name comes from the Latin word "petronius," meaning "of a rock or crag," in reference to its dry and rocky habitat.

Phaeopus phaeopus — **Eurasian whimbrel.** This wader is widespread across much of Asia and Europe. Its scientific name comes from the Greek words "phaios," meaning "dusky" or "grey," and "pous," meaning "foot," in reference to the greenish-grey color of its feet. The bird's common name comes from the word "whimpernel," a term used in 1530 in England to refer to the bird's "whimpering" call. This species no longer has a tautonymous name and is currently classified as *Numenius phaeopus.*

Phoenicurus phoenicurus — **common redstart.** This small bird, a member of the Old World flycatcher family, can be found in Europe and parts of Asia when breeding, and in sub-Saharan Africa in the winter. Males have a distinctive red-orange belly and tail. "Start" is a Middle English word for "tail," hence the common name. The scientific name comes from the Greek words "phoinix" for "red," and "oura" for "tail."

Pica pica — **Eurasian magpie.** The name "pica" is the Latin word for this specific bird, which is also known as the common mapgpie. More interesting is the history of the word "magpie." The term "pie" is derived from a Proto-Indo-European word meaning "pointed," in reference to the bird's beak, or possibly to its tail. For a time, these birds were simply called "pies." The term "mag" comes from the nickname for the name "Margaret," which was once used in English slang to refer to women in general. Apparently, the bird's call was considered by some to sound like the chattering of a woman, and so the bird came to be known as a "Mag pie."

Pipile pipile — **Trinidad piping guan.** This large, turkey-like bird is known locally in Trinidad as the "pawi." It is mainly arboreal, feeding on fruit, flowers, and leaves. It is currently considered critically endangered. The scientific name comes from the Latin word "pipilare," meaning "to chirp," in reference to the thin "piping" call of species in this genus.

***Pipra pipra* — white-crowned manakin.** This small songbird is widespread in the tropical New World from Costa Rica to northeastern Peru and eastern Brazil. Males have black plumage with a white crown, which can be erected as a crest. Females and juveniles are olive-green with grey heads and throats. Its scientific name is a Greek word for a small bird, but it is unclear to which species this word originally referred. This species no longer has a tautonymous name and is currently classified as *Pseudopipra pipra*.

***Poliocephalus poliocephalus* — hoary-headed grebe.** This aquatic diving bird is found in Australia and Tasmania and gets its common name from the silvery-white streaking on its black head. Its scientific name comes from the Greek words "polios," meaning "grey," and "kephale," meaning "head," in reference to the coloring of its head.

***Porphyrio porphyrio* — western swamphen.** This chicken-sized bird of western Europe and northwestern Africa has bright purple plumage and a red bill. It is one of six species of purple swamphen. The scientific name comes from the Greek word "porphura," meaning "purple" or "dark red." Swamphens were often kept in captivity in ancient Greece and Rome as decorative birds in villas and temples.

***Porphyrolaema porphyrolaema* — purple-throated cotinga.** The scientific name of this bird found in the Amazon rainforest comes from the Greek words "porphura" for "purple," and "laimos" for "throat." Males of the species are mostly black with white chests and vivid purple patches on their throats.

***Porzana porzana* — spotted crake.** This small waterbird breeds in Europe and western Asia and migrates to Africa and Pakistan in the winter. Its scientific name comes from the Venetian word for "smaller crake." The English word "crake" comes from the Middle English word "crak," which comes from

Old Norse "kraka," meaning "crow." This appears to ultimately come from a Proto-Indo-European word that is onomatopoeic of the bird's call.

Puffinus puffinus — **Manx shearwater.** This medium-sized seabird gets its scientific name from the word "puffin," which is an Anglo-Norman word from the Middle English "pophyn." The word "puffin" originally referred to the cured carcasses of the fat, puffy shearwater chicks. These birds were a delicacy as early as 1337. Over time, the term "puffin" came to refer to another seabird, the Atlantic puffin (*Fratercula arctica*), possibly because of its similar nesting habits.

Pulsatrix pulsatrix — **spectacled owl.** This large owl is native to the neotropics and can be found in forests from southern Mexico and Trinidad, through Central America, to southern Brazil and northwestern Argentina. Its white facial markings on an otherwise dark-colored face give it its common name. The primary sound made by this owl is a knocking or tapping sound, and it is known as the "knocking owl" in Brazil. Its scientific name comes from the Latin word "pulsare," meaning "to pulsate," in reference to the owl's rhythmic vocalization. This species no longer has a tautonymous name and is currently classified as *Pulsatrix perspicillata*.

Pyrilia pyrilia — **saffron-headed parrot.** The origin of this South American bird's scientific name is unclear. It may ultimately come from the Greek words "pur" for "fire," and "-ilia" for "relating to," in references to the bright orange, yellow, and red coloring often found on birds in this genus.

Pyrope pyrope — **fire-eyed diucon.** This small, passerine bird of South America is mostly grey in color but has vivid, coral-red eyes. Its eyes are the source of its common and scientific names, with "pur" and "opsis" meaning "fire" and "eye" in Greek.

Pyrrhocorax pyrrhocorax — **red-billed chough.** This bird in the crow family has glossy black plumage and a long, curved, red beak. Its striking appearance has led to it being depicted on numerous postage stamps, including in the Gambia, where the bird does not exist. The scientific name comes from the Greek words "purrhos," meaning "flame-colored," and "korax," meaning "raven." The common name refers to the appearance of its bill, and "chough" is onomatopoeic of its call.

Pyrrhula pyrrhula — **Eurasian bullfinch.** This bird, also known as the common bullfinch, gets its scientific name from the Latinized form of the Greek word meaning "flame-colored." It has a large range throughout Eurasia, and males have bright red-orange and deep blue coloring.

Quelea quelea — **red-billed quelea.** This small African bird with a bright red bill has a name that is difficult to trace with certainty. The bird was originally described and named by Carl Linnaeus in the 1758 edition of his *Systema Naturae* where he gave it the name *Emberiza quelea*. He incorrectly mentioned that the bird originated in India (which he corrected in a later edition), likely because ships returning to Europe from the East Indies picked up birds from the African coast on their voyages home. The bird was reclassified in 1850 to *Quelea quelea*, but the name "quelea" remains something of a mystery because Linnaeus himself did not explain the origin of the name. It is locally called a variety of names in Kwangali ("enzunge"), Shona ("chimokoto"), and others. The scientific name may come from the Swahili name for the bird, "kwelea domo-jekundu," but some sources have suggested that the name came from Medieval Latin "qualea" for "quail."

Radjah radjah — **radjah shelduck.** This bird is found mostly in New Guinea and Australia, and on some of the Maluku Islands. Its scientific and common names come from the Moluccan name for this bird. Both males and females of this species are mostly white with dark wing-tips and a dark "collar" around their necks.

Regulus regulus — **goldcrest.** The scientific name of this small European bird is the Latin word meaning "little king." The goldcrest is a member of the kinglet family of birds (Regulidae), which gets its name from the colored crown on the heads of adult birds. This bird's common name also refers to the colorful golden stripe of feathers on its head. The goldcrest is the smallest European bird at only 3.3 to 3.7 inches in length. This is not the only small bird with a tautonymous name to be known as a "little king"—see *Troglodytes troglodytes*.

Riparia riparia — **sand martin.** This bird, also known as the bank swallow and collared sand martin, is a world traveler. In the summer, its range includes almost the entirety of Europe, the Mediterranean countries, much of northern Asia, and much of North America. In the winter, it can be found in most of South America, large parts of Africa, and parts of the Indian Subcontinent and southeastern Asia. The bird's scientific name comes from the Latin word "ripa," for "riverbank," and means "of the riverbank." The origin of the common name "martin" is less clear. One source indicates that the swallow-like birds now known as martins may have been named for St. Martin of Tours, patron saint of France, whose festival day is November 11, about the time that these birds are said to depart for winter. Other sources say that the name may have been arbitrary and that it has no specific meaning. Adding to the confusion, the name "martin" is not used consistently for Old World and New World birds. In the Old World, the term "martin" is used for square-tailed species and "swallow" is used for fork-tailed species. In the New World, the term "martin" is used for all birds in the *Progne* genus. The *Progne* genus also has an interesting history, as the name comes from the Greek mythological figure Procne, who was transformed into a swallow in order to more easily flee from her husband who was trying to kill her. The Procne myth is a dark one worth reading, and Procne's name is the basis of several different genus and family bird names today.

Rupicola rupicola — **Guianan cock-of-the-rock.** This species of cotinga can be found in South American tropical rainforests. Its scientific name comes from the Latin words "rupes," for "rock," and "cola" for "inhabiting," which refers to this bird's habit of nesting on rock walls. Birds of this species have remarkable half-moon crests on their heads, and males have bright orange feathers.

Sephanoides sephanoides — **green-backed firecrown.** This hummingbird is found in Argentina, Chile, and the Juan Fernandez Islands. Adults of both sexes have bronzy green upperparts and green wings and tails. Adult males have iridescent red-yellow crowns. Its scientific name appears to come from the Greek word "stephane," for "crown" or "diadem," and the Greek suffix "-oides," for "resembling." This species no longer has a tautonymous name and is currently classified as *Sephanoides sephaniodes.* Sometimes the specific name is misspelled to match the generic name.

Serinus serinus — **European serin.** The scientific name for this, the smallest European species in the family of finches, appears to come from the French word "serin" for "canary." The French word might have come from the Latin word "citrinus," meaning "citron-colored."

Spinus spinus — **Eurasian siskin.** The scientific name for this small, black and yellow European finch comes from the Greek word "spinos," which was a name for a now-unidentifiable bird. The common name "siskin" appears to be from a German dialect "sisschen" or "zeischen."

Squatarola squatarola — **black-bellied plover.** This medium-sized bird breeds in Arctic regions and migrates to coasts worldwide when not breeding. Its scientific name is a Latinized version of the Venetian name for some kind of plover bird, "sgatarola." This species no longer has a tautonymous name and is currently classified as *Pluvialis squatarola.*

Suiriri suiriri — **suiriri flycatcher.** This South American bird gets its scientific name from the Guarani language where it is a generic name used for several medium-sized flycatchers of the Tyrannidae family. They are called "flycatchers" because they often catch any flying or arboreal insect they encounter.

Sula sula — **red-footed booby.** This species is a large seabird in the booby family, Sulidae. Adults have red feet, but the color of their plumage varies and includes white and brown. They are found widely in the tropics around the world. The scientific name appears to come from the Icelandic or Old Norse name for a gannet, which is a bird that is closely related to the booby, and this word also refers to a foolish person. This may be because of the bird's ungainly gait on land, or because they are so indifferent to people that it is possible to walk up to one and seize it in the hand. These birds even have a habit of landing on sailing ships where they are easily captured and eaten. The common name "booby" may have a similar origin. This word appears to have come from the Spanish slang term "bobo," meaning "stupid." It is believed that adult boobies had no natural predators on their island homes, which caused them to be unafraid of humans that they eventually encountered.

Sutoria sutoria — **common tailorbird.** This songbird is found across tropical Asia and was immortalized in Rudyard Kipling's "Jungle Book" as the character Darzee. Its scientific name is a Latin word meaning "belonging to a shoemaker," which in turn comes from the Latin word "sutilis" for "sewed together." The name refers to the bird's nest, which is made of leaves folded over leaves in a manner that appears sewn together. This species no longer has a tautonymous name and is currently classified as *Orthotomus sutorius*.

Tadorna tadorna — **common shelduck.** This duck's scientific name comes from the French word "tadorne" for this species. The common name "shelduck" comes from the Old English word "sheld," meaning "variegated" or "multicolored." It is widespread in the Palearctic realm.

Tchagra tchagra — **southern tchagra.** The scientific name of this small passerine bird is apparently onomatopoeic of the bird's call, as interpreted by the French ornithologist who described it in 1800. This bird is found in southern and southeastern South Africa and Swaziland.

Temnurus temnurus — **ratchet-tailed treepie.** This Asian bird is a member of the crow and jay family Corvidae. The common name "treepie" is a combination of "tree," where the bird lives, and "pie," which is derived from a Proto-Indo-European word meaning "pointed," in reference to the bird's beak, or possibly to its tail (see *Pica pica*). Its scientific name comes from the

Greek word "temno," meaning "I cut," and "oura," meaning "tail," in reference to the unusual shape of the bird's tail feathers.

***Tetrax tetrax* — little bustard.** This bird's scientific name comes from Greek and refers to a gamebird mentioned by ancient playwright Aristophanes and other ancient Greek figures. The common name "bustard" is said to be from Latin "avis tarda," meaning "slow bird," but this is the opposite of the bird's behavior because it is a fast runner. Apparently, males make a distinctive call that sounds like "prrt."

***Todus todus* — Jamaican tody.** The scientific name of this bird is the Latin word for a small bird. Local names for the Jamaican tody include "rasta bird" and "robin redbreast." These birds are endemic to Jamaica and can be found all around the island. Their heads and wings are bright green and their throats and bills and bright red.

***Totanus totanus* — common redshank.** This red-legged bird is widespread in temperate Europe. It nests in wetlands and is a somewhat noisy bird. Its scientific name comes from the Italian name for this bird, "totano." This species no longer has a tautonymous name and is currently classified as *Tringa totanus*.

***Troglodytes troglodytes* — Eurasian wren.** The scientific name of this small insectivorous bird is taken from the Greek word meaning "cave-dweller" (literally, "a hole" and "to creep"). This is in reference to the bird's habit of disappearing into small crevices when searching for food, or to the shape of its nest when roosting. The wren is also known as the "kinglet" of the birds, a name associated with the fable of the election of the "king of birds." As the story goes, all the world's birds gathered to decide which of them would be king. After much debate, they agreed that the bird that could fly highest would be made king. On the day of the competition, all the birds took to the sky. The small songbirds quickly became too tired to continue. They were soon joined by the ducks, crows, and many others. Eventually, only the strongest of the eagles remained. The eagle climbed higher and higher until the last of his competition returned to earth. He congratulated himself and began his descent. He was exhausted from the competition and needed to recover. But just as he was falling, he heard a small, bright voice above him saying, "I am king! I am king!" It was the little wren fluttering above him. She had hidden herself among the eagle's feathers and ridden his back into the sky. The eagle was furious and complained that the wren only won through trickery, but the wren answered, "Why is strength and brawn better than cunning? If you have your doubts, name another challenge and I shall win again." New challenges were held and the wren continued to win through her cleverness. The other birds eventually agreed that she could be king, but they would never let her rule them. For that reason, it is said, the wren is afraid of eagles and hawks and hides from them in crevices and bushes.

***Turdus turdus* — song thrush.** Whether this European thrush ever had a tautonymous name is unclear, as there do not appear to be scientific papers assigning such a name. Still, some sources suggest that *Turdus turdus* once referred to what is now *Turdus philomelos*. Of note, the first edition of *Systema Naturae*, which pre-dates formalized binomial nomenclature in zoology, described a bird of the genus "Turdus" with the specific name "Turdus." This might be the origin of the belief that a *Turdus turdus* was once a scientific name. The name "turdus" comes from the Latin word for "thrush," a type of passerine bird. Other tautonymous formations from Linnaeus's 1735 version of *Systema Naturae* that pre-date his 1758 formalization of binomial nomenclature in zoology can be found in the Appendix.

***Tympanistria tympanistria* — tambourine dove.** This pigeon is widespread in African woodlands south of the Sahara Desert. Its scientific name comes from the Greek word "tumpanon," meaning "drum," in reference to the bird's call, which resembles the "du du du du" of a drum. This species no longer has a tautonymous name and is currently classified as *Turtur tympanistria*.

***Tyrannus tyrannus* — eastern kingbird.** The scientific name of this large flycatcher comes from the Latin word for "tyrant." They are called "tyrants" or "kings" because of their aggressive defense of their territory, even against much larger animals like hawks, humans, and livestock. The eastern kingbird was described by Carl Linnaeus in 1758 under the name *Lanius tyrannus*. The genus *Tyrannus* was introduced in 1799 with the eastern kingbird as the type species, creating this tautonym.

Urile urile — **red-faced cormorant.** This bird has glossy greenish-blue and purple plumage, and when breeding, its bare facial skin turns bright orange or red. It is also known as the red-faced shag and the violet shag. It can be found in Japan, the Korean Peninsula, the Kamchatka Peninsula, and the Aleutian Arc to the Alaska Peninsula and the Gulf of Alaska. The bird's scientific name appears to come from the Russian vernacular name of this species and likely shares an etymological relationship with the name of the Kuril Islands.

Vanellus vanellus — **northern lapwing.** This wader can be found in Eurosiberia and is also known as the peewit, the tuit, and the green plover. Its scientific name comes from the Latin word "vannus" for a winnowing fan, apparently in reference to the unusual sound made by the slow flapping of the bird's wings in flight. The common name "lapwing" has also been attributed to the "lapping" sound that its wings make.

Xanthocephalus xanthocephalus — **yellow-headed blackbird.** The name of this striking bird comes from the Greek words "xanthous," for "yellow," and "kephale," for "head." The adult males are black with yellow heads and the adult females are brown with dull yellow breasts. These birds are found in the United States, Canada, and Mexico.

Xenopirostris xenopirostris — **Lafresnaye's vanga.** The scientific name for this black and white, medium-sized bird comes from three Greek words: "xenos," "opsis," and "rostrum," which respectively mean "stranger," "appearance," and "beak." The bird is known for having a "strange looking beak," apparently because of the uptilted shape of the mandible. This bird can be found in southern and southwestern Madagascar.

PART IV:

REPTILES

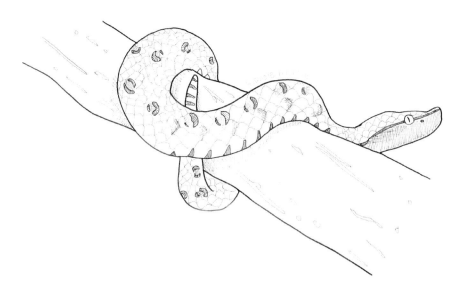

Hypnale hypnale

REPTILES ARE VERTEBRATE ANIMALS GENERALLY characterized by having epidermal scales, being ectothermic, having at least one lung, fertilizing internally, and having four limbs or having descended from four-limbed ancestors. Most are oviparous. The vast majority of reptile tautonyms listed here are members of the Squamata order, which are collectively known as the "scaled reptiles." This order includes over 10,900 species, making it the second-largest order of extant vertebrates after the ray-finned fish of the Perciformes order. Reptiles that are not members of Squamata include turtles, which belong to the Testudines order.

Agama agama — **common agama.** This lizard is also known as the rainbow agama and the red-headed rock agama. Dominant males have striking blue, yellow, and red coloring. The word "agama" has a confusing history. It has been traced to Gbe languages of western Africa as the name for the chameleon and was also used in Dutch Guiana (now Suriname) by imported African slaves who spoke Sranan Tongo to refer to local lizards. The word appears to have no connection to the Greek words "agamos," for "unmarried," or "agamai," for "wonder," as is sometimes suggested.

Ahaetulla ahaetulla — **Andaman bronzeback snake.** This non-venomous colubrid tree snake is found in the Andaman Islands. Its scientific name comes from the Sinhalese name "ehetulla," which means "eye striker" or "eye plucker." This name comes from a widely held but untrue belief that snakes in the genus strike at the eyes of their attackers, blinding them with their pointed snouts. This species no longer has a tautonymous name and is currently classified as *Dendrelaphis andamanensis*.

Ameiva ameiva — **giant ameiva.** This lizard is also known as the Amazon racerunner and the South American ground lizard. With their streamlined bodies and strong hind legs, they can reach speeds of 18 miles per hour. The origin of its scientific name is unclear but appears to be the native name for a lizard from the Tupi language, once spoken by the Tupi people of Brazil.

Basiliscus basiliscus — **common basilisk.** This lizard, found in Central and South America, is also known as the Jesus lizard for its ability to run on the surface of water. Its scientific name comes from the name of the creature of Greek mythology made up of parts of a rooster, snake, and lion, which could turn a man to stone by its gaze. The mythological basilisk was known as a "serpent king," so the Greek basiliskos means "little king." The specific name was given by Carl Linnaeus in his tenth edition of *Systema Naturae.*

Calotes calotes — **common green forest lizard.** This dragon lizard is found in the forests of Western Ghats and the Shevaroy Hills in India and Sri Lanka. Its name is derived from the Greek word "kallos" meaning "beauty." Males develop bright red coloration on their heads and throats during the breeding season.

Caretta caretta — **loggerhead sea turtle.** The loggerhead sea turtle is the world's largest hard-shelled turtle, and it can be found in oceans throughout the world. The scientific name is a Latinization of the French word, "caret," meaning "turtle" or "tortoise." The common name "loggerhead" refers to the animal's unusually large head, which supports powerful jaws that enable it to feed on hard-shelled prey, such as whelks and conchs. Many human activities have negative effects on loggerhead sea turtle populations. The long time required for loggerheads to reach sexual maturity (17-33 years) and the high mortality rates of eggs and young from natural phenomena compound the problems of population reduction as a consequence of human activities.

Cerastes cerastes — **desert horned viper.** The scientific name of this venomous snake of northern Africa comes from the Greek word "keras," meaning "horn," and literally translated means "something horned." The name refers to the pair of supraocular horns on the tops of their heads. A Greek mythological figure known as the Cerastes is named after and based on this animal. The mythological Cerastes is a legendary serpent that is incredibly flexible, has two large horns (or in some myths, four little horns), and ambushes its prey by hiding buried in the desert sand. Leonardo da Vinci wrote the following on the Cerastes: "This has four movable little horns; so, when it wants to feed, it hides under leaves all of its body except these little horns which, as they move, seem to the birds to be some small worms at play. Then they immediately swoop down to pick them and the Cerastes suddenly twines round them and encircles and devours them."

Chalcides chalcides — **Italian three-toed skink.** The scientific name of this animal comes from the Greek word "khalkos," meaning "bronze," and refers to the animal's color. Skinks looks like snakes because of their long tails and cylindrical bodies, but they do have tiny feet. This species of skink has three toes on each foot, as its common name suggests.

Clelia clelia — **mussurana.** The mussurana is a snake native to Central and South America. It is large—with adults reaching a length of 7 feet—and mostly black or grey. It is best known as a snake that specializes in ophiophagy, which is the hunting and eating of other snakes. The mussurana snake kills its prey by coiling around it and constricting it, then swallowing it head-first using special grooved teeth in the back of its mouth. Although they are venomous, they pose no danger to humans. They are immune to the venom of the snakes they feed upon, most notably Central and South American pit vipers. For this reason, farmers sometimes keep mussuranas as pets to keep their living areas clear of pit vipers, which are dangerous to humans and domestic animals. The scientific name is difficult to trace, but it likely comes from the Latin name "Cloelia," which is associated with the word "cluere," meaning "to have renown, fame." This name fits for the mussurana because the snake is so well-regarded among humans. In Sao Paulo, for instance, there is a statue of *Clelia clelia* at a biological research center as a tribute to its usefulness in combating venomous snake bites.

Constrictor constrictor — **boa constrictor.** This nonvenomous snake, also called the red-tailed boa and the common boa, is large and heavy-bodied. It seizes its prey with powerful teeth, then coils around it tightly to stop it from breathing. Its scientific name comes from the Latin word "constringo," meaning "I bind together" or "I compress," in reference to its hunting style. This species no longer has a tautonymous name and is currently classified as *Boa constrictor*. The boa constrictor is one of the few animals whose common name is the same as its scientific name.

Cordylus cordylus — **Cape girdled lizard.** This African lizard and others in the *Cordylus* genus have heavy protective armor, including large spines on their heads, bodies, and tails. The tail can be used as a weapon when it is lashed vigorously from side to side. It is this behavior that gives the Cape girdled lizard its scientific name, which comes from the Greek word "kord-ule," meaning "club" or "cudgel."

Enhydris enhydris — **rainbow water snake.** This mildly venomous snake is endemic to Asia and has several adaptations for life in the water, including eyes positioned on top of its head to see prey and threats while remaining underwater. Its scientific name comes from Greek words meaning "in water," referring to its highly aquatic lifestyle. Although it is not rainbow colored, this snake does have stripes in muted colors running the length of its body, including yellow, olive, brown, cream, and sometimes red.

Gekko gekko — **tokay gecko.** Whether the tokay gecko's scientific name was ever a tautonym is unclear. This colorful, nocturnal, arboreal gecko of Asia currently has a near-tautonymous name, *Gekko gecko*. Lists of its many synonyms do not appear to include any tautonyms. Still, at least one major American natural history museum has the skeleton of a "*Gekko gekko*" on display. The name is believed to come from an 18th century Malay word, "geko," which is imitative of this lizard's unusual, croaking vocalizations.

Hypnale hypnale — **hump-nosed viper.** The origin of the hump-nosed viper's scientific name is difficult to trace. No sources provide the etymology of this snake's name or of the word "hypnale" generally. The word appears to be Greek in origin and bears some similarity with the word "hypnos" for "sleep." This species is a venomous pit viper so one possibility is that the snake's venom puts its victims to sleep or in a sleep-like state. One helpful reference is Edward Topsell's 1608 book, *The History of Serpents*. This work, along with Topsell's *The History of Four-Footed Beasts*, provides a massive, 1,000-page treatise on ancient legends about existing and mythical animals. In his section on asps, Topsell writes: "This Hypnale killeth by sleeping, for after that the wound is given, the Patient falleth into a deep and sweet sleep, wherein it dyeth: and therefore Leonicenus saith; Illam fuisse, ex cujus veneno sibi Cleopatram savem mortem conseivit, that it was the same which Cleopatra bought to bring upon her self a sweet and easie death." Topsell's explanation appears to support the idea that the name "hypnale" describes this snake's sleep-inducing venom. The "hypnale" name was first used to describe these snakes in 1820—long after Topsell's description was published—so it is possible that Topsell's description influenced the taxonomists that named the species a few centuries later.

Iguana iguana — **green iguana.** Also known as the American iguana, this lizard is a large, arboreal, mostly herbivorous species that lives as far south as southern Brazil and as far north as Mexico. Its name is derived from a Spanish form of the Taino name for the species: "iwana." This lizard can grow to an impressive 7.5 feet in length.

Kachuga kachuga — **red-crowned roofed turtle.** This freshwater turtle is endemic to southern Asia. It is critically endangered due to being harvested for meat and shells, drowned in fishing nets, water pollution, and habitat loss. During courtship periods, the heads and necks of male turtles develop bright red, yellow, white, and blue coloration. Its scientific name comes from the Hindi word "kachua," meaning "turtle." This species no longer has a tautonymous name and is currently classified as *Batagur kachuga*.

Mabuya mabuya — **common mabuya.** This skink, also known as the Greater Martinique skink, was once thought to be widespread through the Neotropics but is now understood to be endemic to Martinique. It is feared to be possibly extinct. Its scientific name is a Latinized form of an American Spanish word for "lizard." This species no longer has a tautonymous name and is currently classified as *Mabuya mabouya*.

Naja naja — **Indian cobra.** This venomous elapid is also known as the spectacled cobra and the Asian cobra. Its scientific name is a Latinization of the Sanskrit word "naga"—pronounced with a hard "g"—meaning "snake."

Some argue that the Sanskrit word is a cognate of the English word "snake," but this is doubtful. They say that the Germanic "snek-a-" is similar to the Proto-Indo-European "(s)neg-o-." A more plausible explanation is that "naga" is connected with the Sanskrit "nagna," meaning "hairless" or "naked." The Indian cobra is one of the most widely recognized snakes and is found in India, Pakistan, Bangladesh, Sri Lanka, Nepal, and Bhutan. It is one of the "big four" snakes that cause the most medically significant bites in humans in India. Indian cobras have also been depicted in popular culture, most notably in Rudyard Kipling's "Rikki-Tikki-Tavi," which features a pair of cobras named Nag and Nagaina.

Natrix natrix — **grass snake.** The grass snake, sometimes called the ringed snake or water snake, is a Eurasian non-venomous colubrid. It is often found near water and feeds almost exclusively on amphibians. Its scientific name comes from the Latin word "natare," meaning "to swim," in reference to its strong swimming ability and the fact that it is often found near water. That said, these snakes also spend much time on land and are commonly known as grass snakes. In Baltic mythology, the grass snake is seen as a sacred animal. It was frequently kept as a pet, living under a married couple's bed or in a special place near the hearth. As late as the 19th century in Latvia and Lithuania, there were various folk beliefs that killing grass snakes might bring grave misfortune or that an injured snake will take revenge on the offender. The ancient Baltic belief in grass snakes as household spirits transformed into a belief that there is a snake (known or not to the inhabitants) living under every house; if it leaves, the house will burn down. Common Latvian folk sayings include "who kills a grass snake, kills his happiness."

Ophioscincus ophioscincus — **yolk-bellied snake-skink.** The scientific name of this animal comes from the Greek word "ophis" for "snake," and the Latin word "scincus" for the "skink" family of lizards. Hence the common name, "snake-skink." This species is found in Queensland in Australia and has yellow coloring on its belly.

Plica plica — **collared treerunner.** This lizard is native to the tropical habitats of South America. It is arboreal, meaning it lives most of its life in trees. Its name is derived from the Latin word "plico," meaning "I fold," in reference to the folded skin at the side of its neck. This skin can become distended when the lizard is threatened or angry. For a long time, the *Plica* genus was considered to include only four species, but four new *Plica* species were discovered in 2013. The species count of this genus is expected to increase as there are still several undescribed species. One tribe in the Tucano culture of Colombia holds this lizard in high regard as the mythological "lord of animals" and as a phallic symbol.

Scincus scincus — **common skink.** This animal, also known as the common sandfish, is a type of lizard usually about 8 inches long. Its scientific name is the Latin word for a specific lizard common in Asia and Africa. The common name "sandfish" refers to its adaptations to sandy desert environments. These skinks can move fluidly over sand, and they can breathe even after completely submerging themselves in sand, which they do to prevent overheating and whenever they feel threatened.

Stellio stellio — **starred agama.** This lizard is also known as the roughtail rock agama and the painted dragon. It can be found in Europe, western Asia, and northern Egypt. Its scientific name comes from the Latin word "stella," for "star," in reference to the star-like spots on its body. This species no longer has a tautonymous name and is currently classified as *Laudakia stellio*.

Strophurus strophurus — **western spiny-tailed gecko.** This lizard, like all species in the *Strophurus* genus, is endemic to Australia. They defend themselves from predators by squirting foul-smelling fluid from their tails, which can create a highly flammable substance when mixed with ammonia. The scientific name comes from the Greek words "strophe" and "oura," meaning "turning tail," likely in reference to how this lizard will lift and bend its tail when threatened, revealing brightly colored bands that may act as a warning to predators.

Suta suta — **curl snake.** This venomous snake is an elapid native to Australia. The edges of the snake's vertebral scales can be darker, resulting in a reticulated, net-like pattern from which the Latin name "suta," meaning "stitched," is derived. The common name refers to this snake's defensive posture in which it curls up tightly into a spring-like coil to protect its head.

Tetradactylus tetradactylus — **long-tailed seps.** This lizard can be found in South Africa and its name comes from the Greek words for "four toes or fingers." Interestingly, the *Tetradactylus* genus shows great variation in the number of toes on the feet of the species within it, so the generic name can be misleading. For example, *Tetradactylus africanus* only has one toe on each foot, and *Tetradactylus seps* has five toes on each foot. The tautonymously named species actually does have four toes on each foot.

Uluops uluops — **[no common name].** This extinct species of paracryptodire turtle existed during the Late Jurassic epoch in North America. The species, which is the only member of the genus, is known from a single fossilized skull found in the Morrison Formation in the western United States. Its scientific name comes from the Eskimo word "ulu," for "curved slate knife," and the Greek word "ops," for "face." The name refers to the curved shape of the turtle's upper jaw.

PART V:

AMPHIBIANS

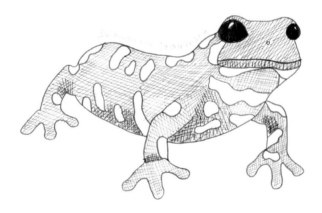

Salamandra salamandra

AMPHIBIANS ARE VERTEBRATE ANIMALS GENERALLY characterized as being ectothermic, having smooth skin, breathing through their skin as well as lungs in some cases, and usually having a complex lifecycle in which they start as larvae. It seems likely that additional amphibian tautonyms exist given that over 8,000 amphibian species have been described, and only five are listed here. One potential reason for the low number of amphibian tautonyms could be that many of the known amphibian species were classified relatively recently. Over 60% of them have been recognized since 1985. More recent descriptions of animals tend to require less reclassification than older descriptions because more recent descriptions can rely upon more up-to-date taxonomic science and modern technology like genetic analysis in making their initial classifications. The reduction in reclassification overall means a reduction in tautonyms caused by reclassification. For instance, when Carl Linnaeus classified the three toads on this list, there were far fewer toad taxons to sort them into and their relationship to other animals was not as well understood as it is today, thus they were all initially placed in the *Rana* genus. They have since been reclassified and given new tautonymous names based on the species names that Linnaeus originally assigned.

Amazops amazops — [no common name]. This limbless, worm-shaped amphibian was first described in 2021. It is a type of caecilian, a relatively small creature that lives hidden in soil or in streambeds in tropical areas and is among the least understood of amphibians. This species was found in Ecuador and is approximately 6.8 inches long and uniformly dark brown. Its scientific name is a combination of the words "Amazon," which is where the type specimen was found, and "opsis," the Greek word for "eye," referring to the unusual bony area around the eye that differentiates this caecilian from others in the Rhinatrematidae family.

Bombina bombina — European fire-bellied toad. This toad is native to eastern parts of mainland Europe and is known for its red belly, which indicates the toad's toxicity and which the toad displays to ward off predators. This toad is also known for having a distinctive "whoop" vocalization. The origin of its scientific name is not clear, but it may come from the Greek word "bombos," referring to the "deep and hollow sound" of the toad's vocal call. Another possibility is that the name comes from a New Latin word for a "bomb" or "explosive," in reference to the vivid red coloring on its belly. Other common names for the animal include the ringing frog, fiery toad, and fire frog.

Bufo bufo — common toad. This animal, also known as the European toad, is found throughout most of Europe, northwestern Asia, and parts of northwestern Africa. Its scientific name is the Latin word for "toad." The origin of the Latin word is not clear, but it may have come from a different Italic language where the word might have referred to any small, creeping animal. A group of toads is often called a "knot."

Pipa pipa — **common Surinam toad.** This unusual toad is almost exclusively aquatic and is almost completely flat. Its hands have long, highly sensitive fingers with star-shaped tips. They lack tongues or vocal cords, instead having bony rods in the larynx that help produce sharp, clicking sounds that travel well through water. They also possess highly modified ears for receiving sound under water. Despite all this, they are perhaps best known for their reproductive habits. A female's eggs, once fertilized, get embedded in small pits in the skin of her back where they incubate. Over time, the embryos develop through to the tadpole stage and erupt from the mother's back as fully developed toads. The origin of its scientific name is difficult to trace but appears to come from the Latin word "pipare," meaning "to peep or chirp," in reference to the toad's unusual clicking sounds. The Surinam toad is often cited as a trigger of trypophobia, an aversion to the sight of irregular patterns or clusters of small holes or bumps.

Salamandra salamandra — **fire salamander.** The scientific name of this European amphibian comes from Ancient Persian and means "lives in fire." This comes from the false belief that salamanders were born in fire or could walk through fire without being harmed. One of the earliest references to this myth was published in Pliny the Elder's *Historia Naturalis*, from the 1st century AD. Pliny threw a salamander into a fire to see if it could survive the flames, as Aristotle had claimed such creatures could. The salamander didn't make it, but that didn't stop Pliny from claiming that salamanders had such powers: "Thus, for instance, the salamander, an animal like a lizard in shape, and with a body speckled all over, never comes out except during heavy showers, and disappears the moment the weather becomes clear. This animal is so intensely cold as to extinguish fire by its contact, in the same way as ice does. It spits forth a milky matter from its mouth; and whatever part of the human body is touched with this, all the hair falls off, and the part assumes the appearance of leprosy." As one might assume from its vivid black and yellow coloration, the fire salamander is poisonous. It can secrete a neuro-toxin from glands in its skin to deter predators. In humans, this can cause skin irritation, muscle convulsions, hypertension, and respiratory paralysis. There is usually no major threat to humans as long as the toxin is not ingested. Still, this has not stopped people from developing another myth about the fire salamander's powers. In the 1200s, an English writer told of a fire salamander laying waste to 4,000 of Alexander the Great's soldiers simply by swimming in a river from which they drank. The many myths of the salamander have continued for hundreds of years, and have been perpetuated by the likes of Leonardo da Vinci, Marco Polo, and others. The salamander even remains a symbol of fire to this day. The origin of the fire myth is unclear but may have started when ancient people would bring moist logs indoors to place them on fires, and the little amphibians who were hibernating in the logs would "mysteriously" crawl out of the logs, appearing to emerge from the flames.

PART VI:

FISH

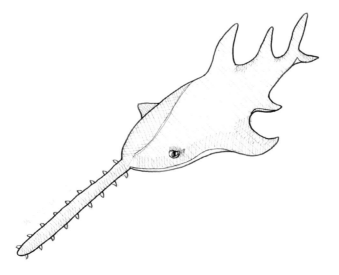

Pristis pristis

FISH ARE VERTEBRATE ANIMALS GENERALLY characterized as being aquatic, gill-bearing, having a skull of cartilage or bone, and lacking limbs and digits. Most (if not all) of the fish species with tautonymous names are members of the Actinopterygii class, known as ray-finned fishes. This is no surprise because actinopterygians constitute nearly 99% of the over 30,000 known species of fish and over 50% of known living vertebrate species. There are also quite a few catfish species on this list, which again is no surprise given that there are over 3,000 known catfish species. Of note, many of the tautonyms on this list resulted from names given by zoologist Francis Buchanan-Hamilton, who described several fishes in India and often used local names for the animals as the basis for their scientific names.

Achirus achirus — **drab sole.** This flatfish is native to tropical and subtropical parts of the Americas. Its scientific name comes from the Greek prefix "a-," meaning "without," and "kheir," meaning "hand," in reference to the fact that this species has no pectoral fins.

Alburnus alburnus — **common bleak.** This small freshwater fish is found in Europe and western Asia. The scientific name is a Latin word meaning, "off-white" or "whitish," likely in reference to the light, silvery color of the fish. In direct sunlight, however, the scales show a wide range of beautiful colors.

Alosa alosa — **allis shad.** This northeastern Atlantic fish in the herring family gets its scientific name from the Latin word "alausa" for "shad." The common name "shad" appears to come from Old English "sceadd" and Old Norse "skata" or Norwegian "skadd," meaning a kind of fish.

Anableps anableps — **largescale four-eyes.** This four-eyed fish is found in the fresh and brackish waters of northern South America and Trinidad. The fish does not actually have four separate eyes, but each of its two eyes is split into two lobes by a horizontal band of tissue, giving each lobe its own pupil and separate vision. This allows the fish to see above and below the surface of the water simultaneously when it swims near the surface. The scientific name comes from the Greek "ana," meaning "up," and "blepein," meaning "sight," in reference to the fish's ability to look up with the upper portion of its eyes.

Anguilla anguilla — **European eel.** This animal's scientific name is a diminutive form of the Latin word "anguis," meaning "snake." The common name "eel" is thought to ultimately come from the second part of the Latin word "anguilla," or "-illa." Eels are distinctive, snake-like fish. There are about 800 species of eel, and they exist in both freshwater and saltwater habitats. Much of the European eel's life history was a mystery for centuries, as fishermen never caught anything that they could identify as a young eel. Unlike many other migrating fish, eels begin their life cycle in the ocean and spend most of their lives in fresh inland water, or brackish coastal water, returning to the ocean to spawn and then die. While this animal's lifespan in the wild has not been determined, captive specimens have lived over 80 years. One specimen known as "the Brantevik Eel" lived for 155 years in the well of a family home in a fishing village in southern Sweden.

Anostomus anostomus — **striped headstander.** The scientific name for this South American fish comes from the Greek words "ano" for "up," and "stoma" for "mouth," in reference to the fish's upturned mouth opening. The common name "headstander" comes from the fact that these fish swim at a 45-degree angle with their heads pointed downwards, as if standing on their heads.

Anthias anthias — **swallowtail sea perch.** This ray-finned fish is native to the eastern Atlantic Ocean and the Mediterranean Sea and is also known as the marine goldfish. The origin of its scientific name is unclear but appears to come from the Greek word "anthias," a name for this or a similar species. Pliny the Elder explained in his *Historia Naturalis* that the "anthias" was difficult to catch because "when they see one of their number taken with a hook, cut the line with the serrated spines which they have on the back, the one that is held fast stretching it out as much as it can, to enable them to cut it."

Argyrozona argyrozona — **carpenter sea bream.** This fish is found in the western Indian Ocean near South Africa. Its scientific name comes from the Greek words "argyros" for "silver," and "zona" for "band, belt," in reference to the five white bands that appear on its body.

Arius arius — **threadfin sea catfish.** This catfish is found in the Indo-West Pacific, including the South China Sea. Its scientific name appears to come from a Latinization of the term "Ari gogora," a local Bengali name for this catfish in India. Some sources attribute the name to the Greek word for "warrior" in reference to its strong dorsal and pectoral fins, but this appears to be incorrect.

Aspius aspius — **asp.** This freshwater fish can be found in Europe. Its scientific name is a Latinization of the word "asp," which comes from the Swedish vernacular for this species, "esp." The name appears to allude to how this fish's spawn run in April coincides with the blooming of aspen trees. This species no longer has a tautonymous name and is currently classified as *Leuciscus aspius*.

Aspredo aspredo — **[no common name].** Females of this small South American catfish carry their eggs attached to the skin on the underside of their bodies until they hatch. The scientific name comes from the Latin word "asper," meaning "rough" or "course," in reference to the appearance of the skin when it is covered in eggs. Members of the Aspredinidae family are known as "banjo catfishes" because their overall body shape resembles a banjo.

Badis badis — **blue badis.** This small, Asian freshwater fish reaches 3 inches in length and is predatory of tiny invertebrates. It is sometimes kept as an aquarium fish. The origin of its scientific name is unclear, but it might come from a local Bengali name for this fish like "bhedo" as the zoologist that described this fish and many others in India, Francis Buchanan-Hamilton, would often give animals names derived from what the native people would call them.

Bagarius bagarius — **devil catfish.** This catfish is found in rivers in southern Asia and gets its scientific name from the Bengali name for the fish, "vaghari." Another catfish in this family, *Bagarius yarrelli*, is believed to feed on human corpses set on fire in funeral pyres in the Kali River in India. It is also believed that *Bagarius yarrelli* have "developed a taste for human flesh" and have attacked humans swimming and bathing in the river.

***Bagre bagre* — coco sea catfish.** This South American catfish gets its name from the Portuguese word for "catfish." It can be found in tropical marine and brackish waters between Colombia and the Amazon River.

***Banjos banjos* — banjofish.** The origin of the scientific name of this fish is uncertain, but it seems to have no connection to the American bluegrass instrument. Instead, the name comes from the caption, "Der Banjos," seen on a page in an 1814 atlas chronicling the round-the-world journey of a Russian explorer named Adam Johann Ritter von Krusenstern. It is not clear where "Der Banjos" came from, but it most likely came from the Japanese name for the fish, "banjos." This, in turn, may have come from the Japanese word, "banzai," an exclamation meaning, "ten thousand years" of long life. Krusenstern's voyage included visits to Japan, but his atlas does not mention why the fish was given this name. The marine ray-finned fish is found in the Indo-West Pacific region from western Australia through Indonesia and the South China Sea to Japan.

***Barbatula barbatula* — stone loach.** This European species of freshwater ray-finned fish lives amongst the gravel and stones of fast-flowing water where it can search for food. The most distinctive feature of this small fish is the presence of whisker-like sensory organs called barbels around its bottom jaw, which this fish uses to detect its invertebrate prey. The scientific name comes from the Latin word "barba," meaning "beard," and refers to the barbels.

***Barbus barbus* — common barbel.** This freshwater fish gets its scientific and common names from the Latin word "barba" for "beard," in reference to the four whisker-like structures on the fish's mouth, which it uses to locate food. The *Barbus* genus has historically been used as a "wastebin taxon" or "catch-all taxon," meaning a collection of organisms that are not easily classified into some other group.

***Batasio batasio* — [no common name].** The name for this catfish appears to come from the local Bengali name for this species, "batashi" or "batasio."

They are found in fast-flowing hillstreams throughout southern and mainland southeastern Asia.

Belobranchus belobranchus — **throat-spine gudgeon.** This fish can be found in fresh and brackish water in coastal streams and estuaries in Indonesia, the Philippines, New Guinea, Fiji, and the Solomon Islands. Its scientific name comes from the Greek words "belos" for "arrow," and "branchus" for "gill," in reference to the unusual shape and positioning of its branchiostegal rays, which make up the membrane covering the gill slits.

Belone belone — **sea needle.** This long and slender fish is also known as the garfish and the garpike. It is found in brackish and marine waters of the Atlantic Ocean, and the Mediterranean, Caribbean, Black, and Baltic Seas. The word "belone" is Greek for "needle" or "needlefish."

Bidyanus bidyanus — **silver perch.** This freshwater fish is endemic to the Murray-Darling river system in southeastern Australia. Its scientific name comes from an Aboriginal name for the species, "bidyan."

Bodianus bodianus — **Spanish hogfish.** This ray-finned fish is found in the western Atlantic Ocean from North Carolina to Brazil. Its scientific name appears to be derived from the Portuguese word "pudiano" for a larger, similar fish. The Portuguese name, in turn, appears to come from the Portuguese word "pudor," meaning "modesty," in reference to the large fish's plain coloring. This species no longer has a tautonymous name and is currently classified as *Bodianus rufus*.

Boops boops — **bogue.** This seabream is native to the eastern Atlantic Ocean. Its common name in most languages refers to its large, bug-like eyes. Its scientific name comes from the Greek word meaning "cow-eye."

Brama brama — **Atlantic pomfret.** The word "brama" comes from the Old French word "breme," meaning a freshwater fish. This fish is also known as Ray's bream and as angelfish, although it is not a true marine angelfish. It is found in the Atlantic, Indian, and southern Pacific oceans, at depths down to 3,300 feet. The common name "pomfret" comes from the Portuguese "pampo," referring to various similar fish.

***Brosme brosme* — cusk.** This North Atlantic cod-like fish is also known as the tusk, torsk, and brosmius. Unlike other cod-like fish, it has only one dorsal fin. The scientific name appears to come from the common name of the species among Danish fishermen of the 18th century, although another source attributes it to the Greek word "brosomai" for "to devour." The common name likely comes from an alteration of Norwegian "tosk" or Old Norse "thorskr" for "codfish."

***Butis butis* — crazy fish.** This sleeper goby is native to fresh and brackish coastal waters of the Indian Ocean and Pacific Ocean from the African coast to Fiji. It is also known as the duckbill sleeper, the upside-down sleeper, the crocodile fish, and the flat-headed gudgeon. The scientific name comes from the local name for this fish near Calcutta, which is believed to have come from the Indian word "buti," which is a decorative circular design on sari fabric that usually contrasts vividly with the background fabric. This is likely in reference to the spots of red on the fish's otherwise dark coloration. The common names "crazy fish" and "upside-down sleeper" refer to the fact that this fish will spend much of its days swimming or hiding in a variety of orientations, including completely upside down.

***Calamus calamus* — saucereye porgy.** This fish is also known as the goat's head porgy and the sugareye porgy and can be found in the western Atlantic Ocean. The origin of the scientific name is unclear. One source attributes it to the Greek mythological figure Kalamos, who allowed himself to drown in a river due to grief and then transformed into an aquatic reed plant in which young saucereye porgies make their homes. Another source states that the name comes from the Greek word "kalamos," meaning a "reed" or "reed pen," in reference to the fish's hollow, pen-shaped second anal-fin spine. The reference to a "reed" appears to be accurate, but the attribution of the reed to the fish has multiple plausible explanations. They have large, round eyes, as their common name suggests.

Callichthys callichthys — **armored catfish.** This subtropical fish found in South America is also known as the cascarudo and the bubblenest catfish. The meaning of its scientific name is unclear. One source attributes it to the Greek words "kalos" for "beautiful," and "ichthys" for "fish." Another source attributes the first part of the name to the Latin word "callum" for "hard skin," in reference to the rows of bony plates running down the length of this fish's body. These plates are the "armor" referred to in its common name. The common name "cascarudo" is Spanish for "hard shelled" or "thick shelled." Males can create bubblenests from plant parts and bubbles formed by their mouths, which is the source of its other common name.

Capoeta capoeta — **Caucasian scraper.** This freshwater fish of western Asia gets its scientific name from the local Georgian and Azeri name for the fish, "kapwaeti." It is a cyprinid, otherwise known as a carp or minnow.

Carassius carassius — **crucian carp.** This medium-sized fish is common in northern European regions. Its scientific name appears to be a Latinization of Low German "karusse," "karass," or something similar, which may have come from Medieval Latin "coracinus" for a kind of river fish.

Catla catla — **catla.** This freshwater fish is also known as the major South Asian carp. Its scientific name comes from the local Bengali, Hindi, and Punjabi names for this species. The fish has somewhat recently been reclassified to the *Labeo* genus, making its current scientific name *Labeo catla*, which is not a tautonym.

Catostomus catostomus — **longnose sucker.** This freshwater fish is native to North America and is also found in Russia. Its scientific name comes from the Greek words "kata," meaning "down," and "stoma," meaning "mouth," in reference to this fish's mouth, which is on the bottom (ventral) side of the fish's head.

Chaca chaca — **frogmouth catfish.** These unusual fish have a sedentary life-style and spend much of their time motionless. They have elongated, broad, and flattened heads, and are also known as squarehead catfish. Apparently, the name "chaca" is a local Assamese name for this fish in India, and it comes from the fact that when removed from the water, the fish will rapidly repeat the sound "chaca."

Chandramara chandramara — **Asian cory.** This species of catfish is native to Bangladesh and India. The scientific name of this fish is difficult to trace, but might come from Chandragupta Maurya, a king of northern India and founder of the Maurya empire, one of the largest empires on the Indian subcontinent.

Chanos chanos — **milkfish.** The scientific name of this fish comes from the Greek word "chanos," or possibly "chasma," referring to an "open mouth," likely in reference to how the fish sometimes feeds at the surface of the water. It is found in the Indian Ocean and the Pacific Ocean, and it is also known as "awa" (in Hawaii), "ava" (in Tahiti), "bangus" (in the Philippines), and "bolu" (in Indonesia). The common name comes from the fact that the fish has a white, flaky meat that resembles the color of milk when cooked.

Chitala chitala — **Indian featherback.** This fish lives in fresh and brackish waters in southern Asia and is also known as the Indian knifefish, a name that refers to the fish's slim body and unusual, curved back. The name "feath-erback" is a reference to the small and narrow dorsal fin, also on the fish's back. The scientific name comes from the Bengali local name for this species.

Chromis chromis — **damselfish.** This ray-finned fish of the eastern Atlantic Ocean and Mediterranean Sea appears to get its scientific name from the Greek word "chromis," which comes from "chremetizein," meaning "to whinny, neigh." It appears that a different species of fish was known as the "chromis" because of its ability to produce sounds with its stomach muscles. This name was later applied to this damselfish and other perch-like fishes once thought to be related. Note that the Greek word "chromis" appears to refer to sounds broader than just "whinny, neigh," as it is used in Homer's *Iliad* to describe the grinding jaws of men in a boxing match.

***Coelorhynchus coelorhynchus* — hollowsnout grenadier.** This silvery-colored fish, also known as the blackspot grenadier, is found in the Atlantic Ocean and Mediterranean Sea. Its scientific name comes from the Greek words "koilos," meaning "hollow," and "rhynchus," meaning "snout," referring to the cavernous mucous chambers in its head. This species has also been known by the tautonymous names *Caelorhynchus caelorhynchus* and *Caelorinchus caelorinchus*. It no longer has a tautonymous name and is currently classified as *Coelorinchus caelorhincus*.

***Conger conger* — European conger.** This species is the heaviest eel in the world and is native to the northeastern Atlantic Ocean, including the Mediterranean Sea. It has been recorded at 9.8 feet in length and 350 pounds. They usually live among holes in rocks known as "eel pits" and they come out at night to hunt and scavenge. Its name comes from the Greek name for the conger eel, "gongros."

***Conta conta* — Conta catfish.** This river catfish of southern Asia is small at only 3.1 inches in length. It occurs in rocky streams in India and Bangladesh. Its scientific name is a Latinized version of the local Bengali name for this species.

***Crenidens crenidens* — karanteen seabream.** This seabream species is found in the western Indian Ocean in shallow coastal waters. Its scientific name comes from the Latin words "crenulatus," meaning "notched," and "dens," meaning "teeth," in reference to the unusual shape of its teeth.

***Cryptocentrus cryptocentrus* — ninebar prawn goby.** This small, ray-finned fish is found in tropical waters, and it has nine white stripes on its body, giving it its common name. Its scientific name comes from the Greek words "kryptos" for "hidden," and "kentron" for "sharp point," referring to a hidden point on its preopercle.

***Cynoglossus cynoglossus* — Bengal tonguesole.** This tonguefish is found in the Indian Ocean in brackish water. The name "tonguefish" refers to their unusual appearance—their bodies are flat, they lack pectoral fins, and their eyes are on the left side of their bodies. The scientific name comes from the Greek words "kyon" for "dog," and "glossa" for "tongue," in reference to the fish's body shape apparently resembling a dog's tongue.

***Dactylopus dactylopus* — fingered dragonet.** This ray-finned fish is widespread throughout the tropical waters of the central Indo-Pacific region. Its scientific name comes from the Greek words "dactylos," meaning "finger," and "pous," meaning "foot." This refers to the first ray of its pelvic fin, which is separate and extended like a finger.

***Dario dario* — scarlet badis.** This tropical freshwater fish is a micropredator at no more than 2 centimeters long. It is found in India and is popular as an aquarium fish. Its scientific name appears to be a Latinized version of the local Bengali name for this species, "darhi."

***Dentex dentex* — common dentex.** This meter-long fish is common in the Mediterranean Sea and has rows of large, well-developed teeth in each jaw. Its scientific name comes from the Latin word "dens" for "teeth."

***Dermatolepis dermatolepis* — leather bass.** This ray-finned fish is a grouper found in the eastern Pacific Ocean. Its scientific name comes from the Greek words "dermatos" for "skin," and "lepis" for "scale," referring to the small scales embedded in its skin.

***Devario devario* — Bengal danio.** This small subtropical fish in the minnow family is found in rivers and ponds in India, Nepal, Bangladesh, Pakistan, and Afghanistan. Its scientific name is a Latinized form of the local Bengali name for this species, "debari."

***Erosa erosa* — pitted stonefish.** This venomous ray-finned fish is also known as the Pacific monkey-fish. It is found in the eastern Indian Ocean and the western Pacific Ocean. It has a large head with bony humps above its eyes, and its coloring varies from reddish to orange or brown mottled with white. Its scientific name comes from the Latin word "erosus" meaning "gnawed" or "eaten away," in reference to the dimpled surface of its bones.

***Erythrinus erythrinus* — red wolf fish.** This small freshwater fish of South America has a reddish-brown coloration. Its scientific name comes from the Greek word "erythros," meaning "red," in reference to its color.

***Flesus flesus* — European flounder.** This flatfish is found in European coastal waters from the White Sea in the north to the Mediterranean Sea in the south. It is usually right-eyed with an underside that is pearly-white, giving it the common name "white fluke." Its scientific name appears to be a Latinization of "flez," a local name for this flounder in France dating to 1558. This species no longer has a tautonymous name and is currently classified as *Platichthys flesus*.

***Gagata gagata* — Gangetic gagata.** This sisorid catfish inhabits fast-moving waters in Bangladesh, Myanmar, and India. The scientific name comes from the local Bengali name for this species in India, "kenyakatta." Its common name refers to the Ganges River, where the fish can be found.

***Galeus galeus* — tope shark.** This houndshark, also known as the snapper shark or school shark, is found worldwide in temperate seas. Although it is widely distributed, this shark is critically endangered because it is targeted by humans for its liver oil, flesh, and fins for food. Its scientific name comes from the Greek word "galeos," meaning a small shark or dogfish. This word might also be translated as "weasel," in which case it would refer to the shark's relatively small body, pointed snout, and swift movements. Note that another tautonymously named houndshark appears to get its name from a word for "weasel"—*Mustelus mustelus*. The tope shark no longer has a tautonymous name and is currently classified as *Galeorhinus galeus*.

***Genidens genidens* — guri sea catfish.** This catfish is found in southern South American rivers. Its scientific name comes from the Greek word "genys" for "jaw," and the Latin word "dens" for "teeth," referring to the moveable teeth in the mouth of this species.

Glyphis glyphis — **speartooth shark.** This rare species of river shark inhabits the coastal marine waters of large tropical rivers in northern Australia and New Guinea. This robust, grey shark has a broad snout, small eyes, a large second dorsal fin, and a black spot beneath each pectoral fin. It grows to about 8.5 feet long. It has large, triangular, serrated teeth in the upper jaw, and narrow, spear-like teeth in the lower jaw that flare outward like an arrowhead before coming to a sharp point. The scientific name appears to come from the Greek word "glyphe" for "carving," in reference to the shape of its teeth, which may appear to have been carved. Alternatively, the source word "glyphe" might be a reference to the knife-like sharpness of the teeth, as knives are used for carving. This species and other river sharks remain poorly known to science because of their secretive habits, and they are facing a critically endangered status since they are so poorly studied. One of the primary threats to this species appears to be habitat degradation, including from human development, pollution, and fishing.

Gobio gobio — **gudgeon.** This small freshwater fish is found in lakes and streams across central and temperate Eurasia. The scientific name appears to come from the Greek word "kobios" for a kind of fish and became the Latin word "gobius" for a gudgeon. Another source suggests that the Greek word likely means "head," in reference to the small fish's large head.

Gonorynchus gonorynchus — **mousefish.** This fish found on temperate continental shelves worldwide is also known as the ratfish, sandfish, and sand eel. The scientific name of this fish comes from the Greek words "gonio," meaning "angle, corner," and "rhynchus," meaning "snout," in reference to the angular nose that these fish use to dig themselves into sand.

Guavina guavina — **sleeper goby.** This ray-finned goby is found in the western Atlantic Ocean from the southeastern United States to Brazil. Its scientific name is the Spanish name for this species and for other sleeper gobies as reported by a Portuguese-Cuban naturalist in 1787.

Hara hara — **kosi hara.** This small, river catfish of southern Asia presumably gets its scientific name from a local Bengali name for this species. Some of its common names appear to be "gagot" and "kutakanti" in Bengali, and "hara" in Finnish and Khasi.

Hemilepidotus hemilepidotus — **red Irish lord.** The scientific name of this brightly colored northern Pacific sculpin comes from the Greek words "hemi," meaning "half," and "lepidotus," meaning "scaled," in reference to the fish's body, which is partially scaled and partially scaleless. As their common name suggests, they are red in color, and have brown, white, and black mottling. They use their coloring to hide camouflaged among rocks on the ocean floor before lashing out to seize their prey of crabs, fish, and shrimp.

Hippocampus hippocampus — **short-spouted seahorse.** The scientific name of this Mediterranean and northern Atlantic seahorse comes from the Greek words for "horse" and "sea-monster." The hippocampus portion of the human brain is so named because of its physical resemblance to a seahorse. Seahorses are the only animal species in which the male bears the unborn young, which frees the female to make more eggs immediately and so to reproduce quicker.

Hippoglossus hippoglossus — **Atlantic halibut.** This flatfish is native to the temperate and arctic waters of the northern Atlantic. It is the largest flatfish in the world, reaching lengths of up to 15 feet and weights of 710 pounds. It can reach 50 years of age. The scientific name comes from the Greek words "hippos," meaning "horse," and "glossa," meaning "tongue," in reference to the large, flat body of the fish. Note that this is not the only tautonymously named flatfish to be named after another animal's tongue—see *Cynoglossus cynoglossus.*

Histrio histrio — **sargassum fish.** This strange-looking fish is found in tropical and subtropical seas in parts of the Atlantic Ocean and the Indo-Pacific

Ocean. Its coloration is usually mottled with yellow, green, and brown on a pale background, and its fins often have dark streaks. The fish can change color from light to dark and its fins are covered in many weed-like protrusions. The scientific name comes from the Latin word "histrio" for "actor" or "harlequin," likely in reference to the fish's colorful and complex pattern, which is reminiscent of the Harlequin character in 16th century Italian theatre that wore a colorful, checkered costume. Another source attributes the name "histrio" or "actor" to the fish's feeding behavior. As an anglerfish, it dangles its front fin ray (known as an esca) as a fishing lure to attract its prey toward its face before darting forward to grab its prey. The scientific name was given by Carl Linnaeus in 1758 at the same time that Linnaeus named the harlequin duck *Anas histrionica* (now *Histrionicus histrionicus*) in reference to the duck's colorful plumage. This suggests that Linnaeus may have been thinking of this fish's coloration, and not its behavior, when giving it a similar Latin name.

Hucho hucho — **Danube salmon.** This freshwater fish is endemic to the Danube basin in Europe where the remaining population is threatened by river damning and overfishing. The scientific name appears to be a Latinization of the local German name for this species, "huchen."

Huso huso — **beluga sturgeon.** This large fish can be found in the Caspian and Black Sea basins and can grow to a size of over 23.5 feet and 3,463 pounds. It is not related to the beluga whale, but both animals get their common name from the Russian word "belyj," meaning "white." For the beluga sturgeon, this is likely in reference to the pale color of the sturgeon's belly as compared to other sturgeons. The scientific name of this fish is the Latin word for "sturgeon."

Idus idus — **ide.** This freshwater fish is found in larger rivers and lakes of northern Europe and Asia. The scientific and common names come from the Swedish "id," meaning "shine," and refer to the fish's bright, whitish color.

This species no longer has a tautonymous name and is currently classified as *Leuciscus idus*.

Lactarius lactarius — **false trevally.** This coastal fish is native to the Indian Ocean and the western Pacific Ocean. The scientific name comes from the Latin word "lac" for "milk." It is unclear why the fish would have this name. One source states that the local name in Pondicherry, India, translates to "peach milk" in reference to the delicacy of its flesh. The common name refers to a different fish, the trevally, which looks similar to and inhabits some of the same waters as this species.

Lagocephalus lagocephalus — **ocean puffer.** This pufferfish is found in all tropical and subtropical oceans and is thought to be responsible for fatal poisonings and should not be eaten. The scientific name comes from the Greek words "lagos" for "hare," and "kephale" for "head," but it is unclear why the ocean puffer has this name. One source suggests that the name refers to the fish's powerful, hare-like incisor teeth.

Lepadogaster lepadogaster — **shore clingfish.** This small fish is found in the Mediterranean Sea. Clingfish are so named because of their habit of clinging to rocks, algae, and seagrass leaves with a sucking disk structure on their chests. The scientific name of this species appears to come from the Greek words "lepas" for "limpet," and "gaster" for "stomach," in reference to the adhesive disk on the fish's belly that allows it to adhere to stones like a limpet or perhaps is shaped like a limpet's conical shell.

Lepidion lepidion — **Mediterranean codling.** This cod-like fish is found in the Mediterranean Sea. Its scientific name comes from the diminutive form of the Greek word "lepis," meaning "scale," in reference to the fish's small, smooth scales.

Leuciscus leuciscus — **common dace.** This ray-finned fish can be found in fresh and brackish water and is native to Europe. Its scientific name is the Greek word for "chub," which is another common name for this and similar species. The Greek word likely comes from "leukos," meaning "white," in reference to the silvery sides of these fish. The common name "dace" likely comes from an Old French or Medieval Latin word for "dart," in reference to the fish's swiftness.

Limanda limanda — **common dab.** This righteye flounder is a flatfish native to the northern Atlantic and Pacific oceans. The scientific name comes from the Latin word "lima" meaning a "carpenter's file," likely in reference to the flat, course appearance of the fish. Like many flatfish, both eyes lie on one side of its head.

Liparis liparis — **common seasnail.** This small marine fish is a member of the seasnail family, a group of fish with long, tadpole-like bodies that is poorly studied. These fish are scaleless with loose, gelatinous skin resembling a snail. The scientific name comes from the Greek word "liparos" for "fatty" or "sleek-skinned," in reference to the fish's smooth, scaleless body. One of the reasons that these fish are not well-studied is because deep-sea species tend to implode when they are brought to the surface.

Lithognathus lithognathus — **white steenbras.** This species is endemic to South Africa and is critically endangered due to overfishing. The scientific name comes from the Greek words "lithos" for "stone," and "gnathos" for "jaw," in reference to the fish's jaw bones (maxillaries) appearing large and solid like stones.

Lota lota — **burbot.** This species is also known as the maria, freshwater cod, lawyer, eelpout, and coney-fish. As one of its common names suggest, it is the only freshwater cod. The common name "burbot" comes from the Latin word "barba," meaning "beard," in reference to the single barbel on its chin. The common name "lawyer" is thought by some to refer to its slimy skin and slippery nature. The scientific name likely comes from the Old French word "lotte" for "codfish," although another source indicates that the word "lota" is an ancient name for some kind of fish. The burbot is something of an enigma—it looks like a cross between a catfish and an eel with a serpent-like body and a single barbel. It uses this barbel to probe the mud for its prey.

Lucioperca lucioperca — **zander.** This ray-finned fish, also known as the sander or pikeperch, is found in fresh and brackish waters in western Eurasia. Its scientific name comes from the Latin word "lucius" for "pike," and the Greek word "perca" for "perch," in reference to its pike-like shape. This species no longer has a tautonymous name and is currently classified as *Sander lucioperca.*

Lutjanus lutjanus — **bigeye snapper.** This marine ray-finned fish is native to the Indian Ocean and the western Pacific Ocean. It is also known as the bigeye seaperch, the rosy snapper, and the yellow snapper. The scientific name is derived from a local Indonesian or Malay name for snappers, "ikan lutjang."

Maena maena — **blotched picarel.** This ray-finned fish with blue-grey coloring and silvery sides is native to the eastern Atlantic Ocean and the Mediterranean Sea. Its scientific name is a Latinization of the ancient Greek name for this or a related species, "maenis." This species no longer has a tautonymous name and is currently classified as *Spicara maena.*

Mastacembelus mastacembelus — **Euphrates spiny eel.** This spiny eel is native to Asia. Its scientific name is difficult to trace, but it might come from the Greek words "mastax," meaning "jaw," and either "embolus," meaning "wedge," or "belos," meaning "arrow," in reference to the pointed shape of the eel's jaw.

Menidia menidia — **Atlantic silverside.** This small fish from the western Atlantic Ocean is a fast swimmer and its silver and white coloration makes it hard for predators to determine which way it is swimming. The scientific name comes from the Greek word "mene," meaning "moon," in reference to the silvery-white of its scales that resemble moonlight.

Merluccius merluccius — **European hake.** This predatory species found in the eastern Atlantic, including in the Mediterranean Sea, is also known as the Cornish salmon. The fish's scientific name comes from the Latin words "mar" for "sea," and "lucius" for "pike."

Microperca microperca — **least darter.** This freshwater ray-finned fish—a type of perch—is found in lakes and streams in the northeastern part of the United States. Its scientific name comes from the Greek words meaning "small perch" in reference to this fish's small size. This species no longer has a tautonymous name and is currently classified as *Etheostoma microperca*.

Microstoma microstoma — **slender argentine.** This fish is found in tropical and subtropical areas around the world. Its scientific name comes from the Greek words for "small mouth."

Mogurnda mogurnda — **northern trout gudgeon.** This colorful freshwater fish native to northern Australia and New Guinea is also known as the northern purple-spotted gudgeon and the Australian spotted gudgeon. Its scientific name is the Aboriginal name for this fish in Australia.

Mola mola — **ocean sunfish.** The ocean sunfish can be found in temperate and tropical waters of every ocean in the world. It is the heaviest of all bony fishes and has a flat, tall body. Its scientific name, "mola," is Latin for "millstone," which the fish resembles because of its grey color, rough texture, and rounded body. (A millstone is a large, circular stone used for grinding grain.) Its common English name, sunfish, refers to the animal's habit of sunbathing at the surface of the water. Its common names in Dutch, Portuguese, French, Spanish, Catalan, Italian, Russian, Greek, Norwegian, and German mean "moon fish," in reference to its rounded shape. In German, the fish is also known as the "swimming head." In Polish, its name means "head alone" or "only head," because it has no true tail. In Swedish, Danish, Norwegian, Dutch, and Finnish, it is also known as the "lump fish." The Chinese translation of its scientific name means "toppled wheel fish."

Molva molva — **common ling.** This fish, also known as the white ling, is a cod-like fish that is found in the northern Atlantic Ocean. It is a large fish, growing up to 6.5 feet in length. Its scientific name is a bit of a mystery. One source states that it comes from the Latin "morua" for "codfish," while another source attributes it to the Breton "mor," meaning "sea," and the Old French "luz," meaning "pike." The common name likely comes from an Old Norse or Germanic word, "langa" or "leng," meaning "long," in reference to the fish's long, slender body.

Mora mora — **common mora.** This deep-sea fish can be found worldwide and is also known as the goodly-eyed cod in reference to its large eyes. Its scientific name comes from the vernacular name for this species in France and Italy, "moro," which presumably comes from the Latin word "morrhua" for "cod." This species no longer has a tautonymous name and is currently classified as *Mora moro*.

Mustelus mustelus — **common smooth-hound.** This dogfish, or "hound-shark," is a type of shark that aggregates in large numbers like a pack of dogs. The scientific name "mustelus" comes from the Latin word "mustela," meaning "weasel." This may be in reference to animal's slender body and its small to medium size. The common smooth-hound is found in the eastern Atlantic Ocean from the British Isles to South Africa, and in the Mediterranean Sea, Madeira, and the Canary Islands.

Myaka myaka — **myaka.** This small fish only grows up to 2.6 inches long and is endemic to Lake Barombi Mbo in western Cameroon. It is critically endangered due in large part to pollution from human activities. Each part of its scientific name is half of the word "myakamyaka," which is the native Barombi name for this species. This is a rare instance where a common name for an animal—myakamyaka—is identical to its complete scientific name—*Myaka myaka*—because it contains both the generic and the specific names. If the scientific name for this fish had been based on the full native word instead of just half of that word, then its scientific name would be *Myakamyaka myakamyaka*, which is a lot of myakas.

Nandus nandus — **Gangetic leaffish.** This Asian leaffish is found in slow-moving or stagnant waters of southern Asia and Indochina. It is also known as the mottled nandus and the mud perch. Its scientific name comes from the local Bengali name, "nanda," for a type of fish, but it is not clear whether that word originally referred to this species or to some other species.

Nangra nangra — **kosi nangra.** This freshwater ray-finned catfish is found in India, Pakistan, Bangladesh, and Nepal. Its scientific name presumably comes from a local Bengali name for this fish. *Nangra* fish are distinguished from other Asian catfish by having barbels that extend beyond the base of the pectoral fins and having very long nasal barbels that are longer than their eye diameter. In lay terms, they are the Asian catfish with the largest beards.

Notopterus notopterus — **bronze featherback.** This ray-finned fish of southern and southeastern Asia is found in fresh and brackish water. Young individuals are dark bronze in color and they get lighter with age. Their common name refers to their coloration and their small, feather-like dorsal fin. The scientific name comes from the Greek words "noton," meaning "back," and "pteron," meaning "wing," in reference to the small dorsal fin.

Oplopomus oplopomus — **spinecheek goby.** This small goby is native to the Indo-Pacific region and is covered in numerous iridescent dots in pale blue, violet, and yellow giving it an unusual glow in certain lighting. The scientific name comes from the Greek words "hoplin" for "weapon," and "poma" for "cover," in reference to the few small spines on its preopercular margins (cheeks).

Oxygaster oxygaster — **knife barb cyprinid.** This medium-sized freshwater fish is found in rivers of southeastern Asia. Its scientific name comes from the Greek words "oxy" for "sharp," and "gaster" for "belly," in reference to the knife-like ridge on the fish's abdomen. This species no longer has a tautonymous name and is currently classified as *Oxygaster anomalura*.

Pagrus pagrus — **red porgy.** This marine ray-finned fish is found in shallow waters on either side of the Atlantic Ocean and is also known as the common seabream. The scientific name comes from the Greek word "phagros," a name for porgies. The common name "porgy" likely comes from this word as well. It appears that the Greek "phagros" comes from a Proto-Indo-European word for "sharpening" because of the pointed shape of the fish's body, or from its sharp teeth.

Panchax panchax — **blue panchax.** This freshwater fish is native to southern Asia and is found in a large variety of habitats due to its high adaptability. It is also known as the whitespot because of a white-colored spot on its head. It helps control mosquito populations by staying near the surface of the water and feeding on mosquito larvae. Its scientific name comes from the local Bengali name for this species in India, "pangchak." This species no longer has a tautonymous name and is currently classified as *Aplocheilus panchax*.

Pangasius pangasius — **Pangas catfish.** This species of shark catfish is native to fresh and brackish waters of Bangladesh, India, Myanmar, and Pakistan. It grows to a standard length of 9.8 feet. The scientific name is a Latinized version of "pangas," the Assamese name for this fish in India.

Phoxinus phoxinus — **Eurasian minnow.** This small freshwater fish in the carp family is also known as the common minnow. It is ubiquitous throughout much of Eurasia in cool streams, lakes, and ponds. It is known for shoaling in large numbers. It is normally only about 3 inches in length. Its scientific name comes from the Greek word "phoxinos" for minnow, which likely came from "phoxos" for "pointed, tapered" in reference to the fish's body.

Phycis phycis — **forkbeard.** This species of hake is native to the Atlantic Ocean and lives on hard and muddy bottoms close to rocks. The scientific name comes from the Greek word "phykon," meaning "seaweed," in reference to fact that the fish lives hidden among seaweeds. The common name refers to their long pelvic-fin rays that look like two strands of a thin beard.

Pinjalo pinjalo — **pinjalo snapper.** This marine ray-finned fish is found in the Indian and western Pacific oceans. Its scientific name comes from the local Malay name for this fish, "ikan pinjalo."

Pollachius pollachius — **pollack.** This marine fish is common in the northeastern Atlantic. Its scientific name is a Latinized version of the Anglo-Saxon common name, "pollack." This might have originated from an older Celtic name for the fish, "podlock," "paddle," or "poullok."

Pristis pristis — **common sawfish.** This incredible looking ray is found worldwide in tropical and subtropical coastal regions and is also known as the largetooth sawfish. It is currently considered critically endangered as a result of overfishing and habitat loss. It reaches up to 23 feet in length and has a long, narrow, flat nose lined with sharp horizontal teeth that resembles a saw. The scientific name is the Greek word for "saw."

Pseudobagarius pseudobagarius — **[no common name].** This catfish from southeastern Asia inhabits clear, swiftly flowing streams. Its scientific name refers to the resemblance that this species has to the catfish in the genus *Bagarius*, with "pseudo" coming from the Greek word for "false." The *Bagarius* genus includes a tautonym of its own, *Bagarius bagarius*.

Pundamilia pundamilia — **[no common name].** This species of ray-finned fish is endemic to the Tanzanian portions of Lake Victoria, the world's largest tropical lake. Its scientific name comes from the Kishwahili word meaning "striped horse," in reference to the black and white stripe pattern on males. This species no longer has a tautonymous name and is currently classified as *Haplochromis pundamilia*.

Pungitius pungitius — **ninespine stickleback.** This freshwater fish is found throughout Eurasia and North America. The number of spines on its back can vary from eight to twelve, and it is sometimes called the ten-spined stickleback. Its scientific name comes from the Latin word "pungere," meaning "to prick," in reference to the small spines on its back.

Rama rama — **[no common name].** This catfish is endemic to India and is found in the Brahmaputra River basin. The origin of its scientific name is unclear. It may come from a local Bengali name for the fish. Other possibilities are that it comes from Rama, the seventh avatar of the Hindu god Vishnu, or is a diminutive form of *Chandramara chandramara*—another tautonym that the zoologist who described the *Rama rama* said it strongly resembles.

Rasbora rasbora — **gangetic scissortail rasbora.** This ray-finned fish is found in southern Asia. Its scientific name appears to come from a local Bengali name for this species. Its common name refers to its deeply forked tail that resembles an open pair of scissors.

Remora remora — **common remora.** This marine fish found in warm waters of the western Mediterranean and the Atlantic Ocean has a dorsal fin that acts as a suction cup, allowing it to attach to larger animals like sharks, dolphins, and whales. This gives the remora access to a steady flow of food, transportation, and protection. It also gives the remora fast-moving water to bathe its gills, which is important because the remora cannot survive in still water and requires water flowing over its gills to breathe. The remora benefits the host animal by eating some of its parasites, but it creates hydrodynamical drag on the host. The scientific name of this fish is the Latin word for "delay" or "hindrance." This name comes from an ancient belief that these fish could slow or stop a ship from sailing by attaching themselves to its hull. Indeed, Pliny the Elder recounted in his *Historia Naturalis* that Marc Antony was defeated at the Battle of Actium because remoras had attached themselves to his ship and stopped it from moving, causing Antony to lose that pivotal battle, and later, the entire Roman Empire. "Winds may blow and storms may rage, and yet the echeneis [remora] controls their fury, restrains their mighty force, and bids ships stand still in their career; a result which no cables, no anchors, from their ponderousness quite incapable of being weighed, could ever have produced! A fish bridles the impetuous violence of the deep, and subdues the frantic rage of the universe—and all this by no effort of its own, no act of resistance on its part, no act at all, in fact, but that of adhering to the bark! Trifling as this object would appear, it suffices to counteract all these forces combined, and to forbid the ship to pass onward in its way! . . . At the battle of Actium, it is said, a fish of this kind stopped the praetorian ship of Antonius in its course, at the moment that he was hastening from ship to ship to encourage and exhort his men, and so compelled him to leave it and go on board another. Hence it was, that the fleet of Caesar gained the advantage in the onset, and charged with a redoubled impetuosity."

Retropinna retropinna — **New Zealand smelt.** This small fish reaches roughly 5 inches in length and is found only in shallow estuaries and rivers in New Zealand. Its scientific name comes from the Latin words "retro" and "pinna," meaning "backwards" or "backside" and "fin," in reference to a small fleshy nub located halfway between its dorsal fin and tail. This fish is also known as the New Zealand cucumber fish because it smells like a cucumber.

Rhinobatos rhinobatos — **common guitarfish.** This cartilaginous fish is native to the eastern Atlantic Ocean and the Mediterranean Sea. Its scientific name comes from the Greek words meaning "nose" and "ray," in reference to its broad, flat face and shovel-like nose. Its common name is also a reference to the fish's unusual shape. It has a flat body like a ray or a skate, and two dorsal fins like a shark. This species has also been given the tautonymous name *Rhinobatus rhinobatus*.

Rita rita — **rita.** This bagrid catfish is found in southern Asia and grows to almost 60 inches long. It is a bottom-dwelling catfish and inhabits muddy waters of rivers and estuaries. The scientific name comes from a local Bengali name for this species.

Rubicundus rubicundus — **[no common name].** This hagfish is found in the western central Pacific Ocean in the Philippine Sea. Its scientific name comes from the Latin word for "ruddy," in reference to the reddish or pink coloring of this and all other species in the genus.

***Rutilus rutilus* — common roach.** This fish is native to most of Europe and western Asia and can be found in fresh and brackish water. It has a bluish-silvery body, a white belly, and red fins. It also has a large red spot in its iris. The scientific name is the Latin word for "ruddy" or "yellowish red," referring to the color of the fish's fins.

***Salvelinus salvelinus* — lake char.** This fish is found in lakes in the European Alps. It usually inhabits deeper waters of the lakes and feeds on crustaceans and insects. Its scientific name is a Latinization of the German word "saibling," meaning "char" or "little salmon." This species no longer has a tautonymous name and is currently classified as *Salvelinus umbla*.

***Sarda sarda* — Atlantic bonito.** This large mackerel-like fish is common in shallow waters of the Atlantic Ocean, the Mediterranean Sea, and the Black Sea. The origin of the scientific name is unclear. One source states that "sarda" was an ancient name for caught and salted tuna in the waters of western Europe. Another source states that "sarda" refers to the island of Sardinia, one location where the fish can be found.

***Silurus silurus* — wels catfish.** This large species of catfish is native to central, southern, and eastern Europe. It is a freshwater bottom feeder and can live for at least fifty years. Its scientific name comes from the Greek word "silouros" for "catfish." This species no longer has a tautonymous name and is currently classified as *Silurus glanis*.

***Solea solea* — common sole.** This flatfish, also known as the black sole and the Dover sole, lives on the sandy or muddy seabed of the northern Atlantic Ocean and the Mediterranean Sea. Its scientific name is the Latin word for "sandal" or "sole," referring to the flat shape of the fish's body.

***Sphyraena sphyraena* — European barracuda.** This ray-finned predatory fish lives in the Mediterranean basin and the warmer waters of the Atlantic Ocean, and its scientific name comes from the Greek word "sphyraina," an ancient name for a fish. The origin of this word is unclear. One source states that it comes from a Greek word meaning a javelin or a pointed stick, in reference to the slender, sharp-headed bodies of the fish. Another source attributes it to the Greek word "sphura," meaning "hammer, mallet." (The hammerhead sharks are in the family Sphyrnidae.) The word "barracuda" appears to come from the Spanish or Cariban word for this fish.

Spinachia spinachia — **sea stickleback.** This small and slender fish, also known as the fifteen-spined stickleback, lives in brackish waters of the northeastern Atlantic Ocean. Its scientific name comes from the Latin word "spina," meaning "thorn," in reference to its anterior dorsal fin, which consists of fourteen or fifteen widely separated spines.

Sprattus sprattus — **European sprat.** This fish is also known as the bristling, garvie, Russian sardine, and whitebait. It is a small marine fish in the herring family found in European waters. Its scientific name comes from the Old German word "sprotte" for "small fish," or perhaps an Old English word "sprot" for "herring-like fish."

Squatina squatina — **angelshark.** This shark, also known as a monkfish, has a large, flat body giving it a resemblance to a ray or skate. It inhabits the northeastern Atlantic Ocean, though it is currently considered critically endangered. The scientific name for this animal appears to be the Latin word for "a kind of shark." Another source indicates that the name is the Latin word for "skate," in reference to the fish's appearance. The common name refers to the flaps around their heads, which are flattened pectoral fins and look like wings, or perhaps like a monk's habit.

Stellifer stellifer — **little croaker.** This fish is found in the western Atlantic Ocean in marine, brackish, and tropical waters. Its scientific name comes from the Latin words "stella" for "star," and "ferre" for "to bear," referring to the radiated, star-like pattern on the fish's face near its eyes.

Strongylura strongylura — **spottail needlefish.** This needlefish is found in the Indian and western Pacific oceans in coastal waters. Some have even been found living buried in mud during low tides. Its scientific name comes from the Greek words "strongylos" for "round," and "oura" for "tail," likely referring to the round spot marking on its tail.

Synodus synodus — **diamond lizardfish.** This bottom-dwelling ray-finned fish lives in tropical and subtropical waters of the Atlantic Ocean. It is often identified by the dark red stripes on its back. The word "synodus" was first used in Pliny the Elder's *Historia Naturalis* to describe an unknown fish said to have a stone in its brain. The word was later given as the name for this species, presumably because the teeth of this fish's jaws interlock, and the word comes from the Greek "syn" and "odous" meaning "together" and "tooth." The common name lizardfish refers to the fishes' cylindrical bodies, scaly heads, and numerous small teeth, similar in some sense to what lizards look like.

Tandanus tandanus — **eel-tailed catfish.** This freshwater fish native to the Murray-Darling river system of eastern Australia is also known as the dewfish, freshwater catfish, and jewfish. The scientific name comes from an Aboriginal Australian name for the fish, "tandan." The back half of this fish's body tapers into a pointed, eel-like tail.

Tautog tautog — **tautog.** Whether this scientific name was ever assigned to a species is unclear. There appear to be no scientific sources that recognize *Tautog tautog* as a current or former animal name. It appears that this name may have been intended for *Tautoga onitis*, also known as the blackfish or the tautog. If so, this marine fish can be found in the western Atlantic Ocean. The name "tautog" comes from a Native American word for this species.

Thymallus thymallus — **grayling.** This freshwater fish is native to Europe, where it is widespread in the northern parts of the continent. It occurs in cold, clean, running waters, but also appears in lakes and in brackish waters around the Baltic Sea. Its scientific name comes from the Greek word "thymallos" for a kind of fish similar to a salmon. According to European folklore, the name originates from the Greek word "thumon," meaning "thyme," because the flesh of this fish tastes like thyme.

Tinca tinca — **tench.** This fish inhabits fresh and brackish waters throughout Eurasia and is also known as the doctor fish. The common name doctor fish comes from a folklore belief that the slime on the skin of this fish would cure any sick fish that rubbed against it. The scientific name is the Latin word for a tench fish, but its origins are difficult to trace. One source states that the word comes from a Proto-Indo-European word meaning "to melt" because the fish was thought to be poisonous. Another source suggests that the name was derived from a similar name of some predatory fish.

Tor tor — **tor mahseer.** This fish, also known as the tor barb and the red-finned mahseer, is found in the fast-flowing rivers of India, Bangladesh, Nepal, and Pakistan. It is commercially important as a food and game fish. Its scientific name comes from a native word, "tora," for large freshwater carp in the Ganges River system. This scientific name is tied for the shortest tautonym.

Torpedo torpedo — **common torpedo.** This animal, also known as the ocellate torpedo or eyed electric ray, can deliver a strong electric shock of up to 200 volts for attack or defense. It can be found in the eastern Atlantic Ocean and the Mediterranean Sea. It has a disk-like shape and usually has five prominent blue spots on its back. The word "torpedo" was the Roman name for electric rays, coming from the Latin word "torpere," meaning "to be numb."

Trachurus trachurus — **Atlantic horse mackerel.** This species of jack mackerel is also known as the common scad and is found in the eastern Atlantic Ocean off Europe and Africa and in parts of the southeastern Indian Ocean. The scientific name for this species comes from the Greek words "trachys," meaning "rough," and "oura," meaning "tail," in reference to spiny plates on the rear of the fish between its dorsal and anal fins and its tail.

Trachycorystes trachycorystes — **black catfish.** This species of driftwood catfish is found in Brazil, Guyana, and Venezuela. It is also known as the iron head driftwood catfish and the black woodcat. Its scientific name comes from the Greek words "trachys," meaning "rough," and "corystes," meaning "helmet," in reference to its wrinkled and very strong cranial shield.

***Trachyrincus trachyrincus* — roughsnout grenadier.** This species of marine fish is found in the eastern Atlantic Ocean and the Mediterranean Sea. It has a large head and a pointed snout with a ridge on the side. The scientific name comes from the Greek word "trachys" for "rough," and "rhynchus" for "snout," in reference to the rough scales and sharp, ridged snout of this fish. This species no longer has a tautonymous name and is currently classified as *Trachyrincus scabrous.*

***Trichodon trichodon* — Pacific sandfish.** This small, deepwater fish is native to the Pacific coast of North America. Its scientific name comes from the Greek words "trichos" for "hair," and "odon" for "tooth," referring to its thin and sharp teeth.

***Tropheops tropheops* — golden tropheops.** This fish is endemic to Lake Malawi, which is the fifth largest freshwater lake in the world by volume and has more species of fish living in it than any other lake in the world. The scientific name of this fish comes from the Greek suffix "ops," meaning "resembling," because this fish has a similar appearance to fish in the *Tropheus* genus. The *Tropheus* generic name comes from the Greek word "trophos," meaning "to nurse," in reference to the unusual oral incubation behavior of *Tropheus* fish.

***Trutta trutta* — brown trout.** This European species of salmonid fish has been widely introduced to environments throughout the world. It is a medium-sized fish with a slender, reddish-brown body and a long, narrow head. Its scientific name comes from the Latin word for "trout," although the origin of the Latin word is not clear. This fish has over sixty different previous scientific names, known as synonyms. This fish no longer has a tautonymous name and is currently classified as *Salmo trutta.*

Uraspis uraspis — **whitemouth jack.** This jack is found in the Indo-Pacific Ocean from the Red Sea to Sri Lanka and from The Philippines to Hawaii. Its scientific name comes from the Greek words "oura" for "tail," and "aspis" for "shield," likely in reference to the large scales on the part of its body near its tail.

Vimba vimba — **vimba bream.** This European fish, also known as the zanthe, lives in European seas but makes an annual migration up-river to breed. Its scientific name likely comes from the local Swedish name for this fish, "vimma."

Zebrus zebrus — **zebra goby.** This species of goby is native to lagoons and tide pools of the Mediterranean Sea. It has an unusual zebra-like color pattern of whitish transverse bands around a dark body, giving it its scientific name, which is a Latinized version of the word "zebra."

Zingel zingel — **zingel.** This freshwater ray-finned fish is found in fast-flowing streams in southeastern Europe. It usually has dark and light brown splotches of color, giving it some camouflage. The scientific name comes from the German name for this species, which appears as early as 1756 in Wilhelm Heinrich Kramer's work on the flora and fauna of Lower Austria.

Zungaro zungaro — **gilded catfish.** This South American catfish is also known as the manguruyu and the jau. The scientific name comes from the local name in the Amazon region of Peru that is given to large, long-whiskered catfish.

PART VII:

ARTHROPODS

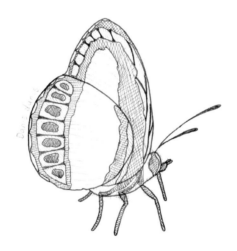

Danis danis

ARTHROPODS ARE INVERTEBRATE ANIMALS GENERALLY characterized by exoskeletons, segmented bodies, and paired jointed appendages. Many of the known arthropod species are beetles and moths. Indeed, beetles and moths collectively make up an estimated 38% of all known species of life and 56% of all known animal species.

The arthropod tautonyms include many skippers, butterflies, and moths, which are part of the Lepidoptera order. Many of the butterflies were originally described by Carl Linnaeaus and given names based on ancient Greek and Roman mythology. Many of the skippers were originally described or reclassified by entomologists William Harry Evans and William Chapman Hewitson, among others. These individuals had their own idiosyncrasies when it came to naming animals. In some instances, Evans named the animals using portions of the locality names where the type specimens were found, as with the *Pamba pamba* skipper collected from Balzapamba, Ecuador. Evans and others also used anagrams when naming species, as with members of the *Venada* genus being named *advena*, *daneva*, and *nevada*, or the species *Venas evans*. Hewitson also appears to have used both anagrams and ancient references in his scientific names.

Many of the proposed etymologies here are speculative, however. This is due in large part to the lack of available information on why names were given and the sheer abundance of tautonymous names for arthropods. Moreover, many of the skippers on this list have similar appearances with only very slight morphological differences, which adds to the difficulty of interpreting the intent behind their names. By contrast, a scientific name that appears to mean "red cheek" and is given to a bird with a red face can reasonably be understood to refer to the bird's physical appearance. Where the animal's physical appearance is indistinct, as with many skippers, that is one less clue at our disposal in understanding the name. For these reasons, the section that follows is perhaps where the greatest value of this book lies, as well as its greatest etymological errors. Every effort has been made to review original descriptions and reclassifications for clues, as well as to examine physical, behavioral, and habitat characteristics of these species, in combination with known naming habits of the entomologists who created the names. The only Latin phrase that should be accepted without reservation here is *Caveat lector*.

***Aecas aecas* — aecas ruby-eye.** This skipper has wings that are medium brown with transparent spots on top and light yellowish-brown with blueish-white metallic colors on bottom. It inhabits areas from Suriname and Brazil to Mexico. The origin of the scientific name is unclear, and there is little information upon which to make a reliable guess. It might refer to Aeacus, the Greek mythological figure who was a son of Zeus and a judge of the dead, or to the ancient city of Aecas that was captured by Hannibal during the Second Punic War. The mythological figure seems like the most likely source given that the entomologist who named it used other mythological figures when naming species in the same publication, including the nymph Psecas, the Greek warrior Sinon, the sky god Coelus, and Poseidon's daughter Evadnes (likely from Evadne). This species no longer has a tautonymous name and is currently classified as *Flaccilla aecas*.

***Aega aega* — [no common name].** Whether a species with this name exists is unclear. Although there are many species within the *Aega* genus, there appear to be no scientific sources that recognize *Aega aega* as a current or former animal name. Assuming this animal exists within *Aega*, it is an isopod, which is a type of small crustacean that includes woodlice. They can be found in the sea, in fresh water, or on land. The origin of the scientific name is unclear, but it might refer to the Greek mythological figure Aega, who nursed the infant Zeus in Crete.

***Aniculus aniculus* — scaly-legged hermit crab.** This aquatic hermit crab is found in the Indo-Pacific Ocean and appears to have legs covered in long red and yellow hairs, which are not really hairs but are extensions of its exoskeleton called setae. The origin of its scientific name is unclear. One source attributes it to the Latin word "aniculus" for "little old man," in reference to its hairy body, reminiscent of that of an old man. This is plausible given that the original description of this animal from 1787 referred to its features as "wrinkled." However, it is also unclear whether "aniculus" was ever a Latin word meaning "little old man." The word "anicula" means "little old woman," but there is almost no indication that the word was used with the masculine gender. Precision is no man's enemy, and a more precise understanding of the historical usage of this word may clarify the etymological origins of this scientific name.

Anthrax anthrax — **[no common name].** This species of fly can be found throughout mainland Europe from May to August. The scientific name comes from the Greek word for coal, likely in reference to the fly's black color. It has six white tufts of hair on its abdomen, which are unique to this species. This fly is fairly large at 10 millimeters in length.

Appia appia — **appia skipper.** This skipper has dark brown wings with light brown and grey spots, and it inhabits Argentina. The origin of the scientific name is unclear, and there is little information upon which to make a reliable guess. The name might refer to a portion of the name of the locality where the type specimen was collected, as was often the case for species named by entomologist W.H. Evans, or it may reflect some other unknown whim of his. For instance, Evans described this species as having a "very short apiculus," which is the hooked tip at the end of a skipper's antenna. Perhaps "appia" was derived from—and represents a "shortened" version of—the word "apiculus." Alternatively, it might refer to some place or person of antiquity as was often done for lepidopteran names, such as the Via Appia or the Appius praenomen of ancient Rome.

Ariadne ariadne — **angled castor.** This species of nymphalid butterfly is found in Asia. It has orange wings with black wavy lines running across. Its scientific name appears to come from the name of the Greek mythological princess Ariadne, who helped Theseus escape the Minotaur's labyrinth. As the story goes, Ariadne gave Theseus a ball of thread, which he unrolled as he walked further into the maze. This allowed him to find his way back out after killing the Minotaur.

Aristyllis aristyllis — **[no common name].** This achilid leafhopper is an insect that, like all leafhoppers and planthoppers, has a remarkable resemblance to leaves and other plants in its environment and "hops" for quick transportation from one plant to the next. This species can be found in Queesland, Australia, and the origin of its scientific name is unclear. It appears to refer to the ancient Greek astronomer Aristyllus, or to some combination of Greek words such as "ari" and "stylos," roughly meaning a "very pointed instrument," or "aristos," meaning "excellence," with a diminutive suffix.

Arita arita — **arita skipper.** This skipper is described as having dark brown wings with white and yellowish spots, and it inhabits Trinidad. It is also known as the green-browed skipper due to a tuft of green hair on the top of its face. The origin of the scientific name is unclear, and there is little information upon which to make a reliable guess. It may refer to a local vernacular for this or another skipper, to a location where it was found, or even to a specific person. For instance, a Brazilian tree used by indigenous people to make tables is locally called "arita," and perhaps in one of these trees is where the first specimen was found. Alternatively, it may be a subtle reference to, or anagram of, some other species name, as the entomologist who first described it, William Schaus, would occasionally use anagrams and other wordplay to name similar species, such as in the skippers *Augiades tania* and *Augiades anita*.

Aroma aroma — **aroma skipper.** This skipper is described as being dark brown with the body and base of the wings being blue-green with a reddish-brown underside. It inhabits Brazil, Peru, and Nicaragua. The origin of the scientific name is unclear, and there is little information upon which to make a reliable guess. It may refer to the ancient Carian town of Aroma, inhabited during the Roman Empire period, or it might refer to the Latin word "aroma" for "spice" or "fragrant smell."

Aspitha aspitha — **aspitha firetip.** This skipper is described as being mostly dark brown in color with reddish-yellow and white banded markings. It inhabits the Amazon River area near the Brazilian states of Para and Sao Paulo. The origin of the scientific name is unclear, and there is little information upon which to make a reliable guess. It may be or derive from the Greek word "aspitha" or "aspida" for "shield." Another possibility is that the name refers to Aspida Hill in Argos, home to an ancient temple and gravesite. The entomologist who named it, William Chapman Hewitson, appears to have named several other species after ancient cities. The common name "firetip" refers to the red tuft at the end of the abdomen for certain species in the Pyrginae subfamily.

Astacus astacus — **European crayfish.** This lobster-like arthropod is also known as the noble crayfish and the broad-fingered crayfish. It is the most common species of crayfish in Europe, and a traditional food source. Its scientific name comes from the Greek word "astacos," meaning "lobster" or "crayfish."

Avicularia avicularia — **pinktoe tarantula.** This spider can be found in trees from Costa Rica to Brazil and the southern Caribbean. An adult pinktoe tarantula can grow up to 6 inches in length. The species was originally named *Aranea avicularia* by Carl Linnaeus in 1758. The name "avicularia" comes from the Latin word "avicula," meaning "little bird," and the suffix "-aria," meaning "pertaining to." This name refers to a 1705 illustration by Maria Sibylla Merian showing a tarantula feeding on a bird. It is rare for pinktoe tarantulas to eat birds, and although Merian's famous picture illustrates a real event that she witnessed in Suriname, it is more likely that the spider was scavenging a dead bird than catching a live one. This was the first depiction of a tarantula to capture the public imagination, and it had an impact on how people saw these spiders. The genus *Avicularia* was erected in 1818 by Jean-Baptiste Lamarck, and Linnaeus's *Aranea avicularia* was moved into it, creating a tautonym.

Baeotus baeotus — **graphic beauty butterfly**. This beautiful butterfly has wings that are black with vivid light and dark blue markings on top, and white with complex black and yellow markings on bottom. It can be found from Mexico to Brazil. The origin of the scientific name is unclear, but it may refer to a Greek mythological figure named Boeotus (sometimes spelled Beotus), son of Posiedon (or, in another story, son of the king Itonus). Alternatively, it might be a Latinized version of the Spanish word for "blessed." The tautonymous name *Baeotus baeotus* appears to have resulted from a misspelling of the original specific name *Megistanis beotus*, which was first published in 1845. The misspelling of "baeotus" appeared in 1850 and continued to be used for decades when, in 1987, the tautonym *Baeotus baeotus* was formed. In 2001, the species was renamed to *Baeotus beotus*, reflecting the misspelling in the generic name and the original spelling in the specific name. As such, it no longer has a tautonymous name.

Balanus balanus — **rough barnacle.** This species of acorn barnacle is native to the colder seas of the Northern Hemisphere. Unlike most crustaceans, barnacles start their lives as free-swimming larvae and are unable to move from place to place once their cement glands affix them to rocks or other surfaces. Its scientific name comes from the Greek word "balanos," meaning "acorn," in reference to its cone-like, symmetrical shape and pale brown color.

Banta banta — **[no common name].** This skipper is described as having dark brown wings with white and yellowish patches underneath, and it inhabits New Guinea. The origin of the scientific name is unclear, and there is little information upon which to make a reliable guess. The name might refer to a portion of the name of the locality where the type specimen was collected, as was often the case for species named by entomologist W.H. Evans, or it may reflect some other unknown whim of his. One potential explanation is that the name comes from part of the word "Angabanga," which is the name of the river in New Guinea where the type species was found. Another is that it comes from the word "banta," meaning "man," in the Gadsup language of the Gadsup people of Papua New Guinea.

Bruna bruna — **[no common name].** This skipper has wings that are uniformly dark brown, and it was originally described as inhabiting "Masun," which likely refers to a part of the Amazon rainforest. The origin of the scientific name is unclear, and there is little information upon which to make a reliable guess. The name might refer to a portion of the name of the locality where the type specimen was collected, as was often the case for species named by entomologist W.H. Evans, or it may reflect some other unknown whim of his. Alternatively, it might come from a Latin or Proto-Germanic word such as "brunaz," for "brown," in reference to its coloring.

Bucayana bucayana — [**no common name**]. This neotropical arachnid is a species of harvestmen, which are also known as daddy longlegs (but are distinct from cellar spiders). Harvestmen are also known as shepherd spiders in reference to how their long legs remind observers of how some European shepherds used stilts to better watch their flocks from a distance. Although they are similar to spiders in appearance, they are members of a distinct order (Opiliones) that is not closely related to spiders, and harvestmen do not build webs. An urban legend associated with harvestmen and other "daddy longlegs" states that these arachnids are highly venomous but possess fangs too short to pierce human skin. This is untrue, as none of the harvestmen have venom glands and they do not have fangs, but pincer-like claws in their mouths. This particular species is within the Cranaidae family, named for the Greek mythological king Cranaus. The scientific name of this Ecuadorian species refers to the town of Bucay in Ecuador, presumably where the type specimen was obtained.

Cactus cactus — [**no common name**]. This water flea is the only species within its genus. Only one specimen has been collected and described (vaguely), and that specimen was found in Chile. Water fleas are small planktonic crustaceans whose swimming style resembles the movements of fleas. The origin of the scientific name of this species is unclear, and there is little information upon which to make a reliable guess. It might come from the Latin word for "cardoon" or "thistle," but the reason for giving such a name is unclear.

Calappa calappa — **smooth box crab.** This tropical species of crab is also known as the red-spotted box crab. Its scientific name comes from the Malay word, "kelapa," meaning "coconut." These crabs show great variability in their patterning and coloration, often appearing with light brown shells resembling coconuts. Crabs of the *Calappa* genus are also generally known as shame-faced crabs because of the way their claws fold up and cover their faces, as if they were hiding their faces in shame.

Caleta caleta — **angled Pierrot.** This butterfly has an upperside that is dark brown with a broad white band, and an underside that is mostly white with several brownish-black markings. It inhabits Sulawesi and the Philippines. The origin of the scientific name is unclear, and there is little information upon which to make a reliable guess. It might be a reference to the ancient Phonecian settlement of Sa Caleta off the eastern coast of modern-day Spain, as it was a habit of entomologist William Chapman Hewitson to refer to ancient city names when naming new species.

Cedusa cedusa — **[no common name].** This small, winged, New World insect is a derbid planthopper. The origin of its scientific name is unclear, and there is little information upon which to make a reliable guess. The entomologist who created this name appears to have used words describing physical characteristics when naming other species like *Cedusa venosa* (Latin for "veins"), so perhaps "cedusa" comes from a Latin or Spanish word for a physical characteristic of this insect. It also bears some resemblance to the Greek word "kedos," meaning "anxiety, grief," although it is not clear why such a word would be used when naming this species. Perhaps more interesting than the origin of this name is the fact that many species within the *Cedusa* genus are named with meaningless words that rhyme with *Cedusa*, including *bedusa*, *gedusa*, *hedusa*, *kedusa*, *ledusa*, *medusa*, *nedusa*, *pedusa*, *redusa*, *vedusa*, and *zedusa*.

Cephise cephise — **cephise skipper.** This skipper is mostly medium brown with light brown or off-white spots on each of its front wings. It is native to Brazil and Peru. The origin of the scientific name is unclear, and there is little information upon which to make a reliable guess. It might refer to Cepheus, the Greek mythological king for whom a constellation is named. Alternatively, it might refer to stem sawflies of the Cephidae family due to a shared resemblance or habitat.

Chaetosiphon chaetosiphon — **[no common name].** This species of European aphid gets its scientific name from the Greek words "chaite," meaning "long hair," and "siphon," meaning "tube, straw." The name likely refers to the small hairs on its body and to its siphunculi, a pair of abdominal tubes that secrete a defensive fluid.

Chalcone chalcone — **brick skipper.** This skipper has wings that are medium brown with vivid yellowish-orange markings, and it inhabits Brazil. The origin of the scientific name is unclear, and there is little information upon which to make a reliable guess. It might come from the Greek word "chalkos," meaning "copper," in reference to the color of its wings. This species no longer has a tautonymous name and is currently classified as *Chalcone briquenydan chalcone*. At one time it was also classified as the misspelled tautonym *Chalcona chalcona*.

Chamunda chamunda — **[no common name].** This skipper has wings that are dark brown with black and white markings, and it inhabits southern and southeastern Asia including India, Thailand, Laos, and parts of Malaysia. The scientific name appears to refer to the Hindu goddess Chamunda, as the type specimen was collected from Bengal.

Clibanarius clibanarius — **[no common name].** This hermit crab inhabits waters off the Indian coast. The scientific name appears to refer to the Clibanarii, an ancient Byzantine military unit of armored cavalry. This name comes from the Greek word "kilbanos," meaning "camp oven" or "metallic furnace," and likely refers to the fact that the men in this miliary unit tended to get hot quickly because of the heavy armor they wore. For this species of hermit crab, the name refers to its tough shell.

Clito clito — [no common name]. This skipper has wings that are mostly black or dark brown with large white markings. It inhabits French Guiana. The scientific name appears to refer to a person or mythological figure of antiquity such as "Clito," the mother of Greek dramatist Euripides, or "Clito," a mortal princess with whom Poseidon had many children. Other antiquity-inspired names given by the same entomologist in the same genus and publication include "mennipus" (Greek warrior in the Trojan War), "talaus" (king of Argos), "phocion" (ancient Athenian stateman), "iupiter" (Roman equivalent of Zeus), and "virbius" (alter ego of Hippolytus and son of Theseus), the latter of whom was the subject of a famous tragic work by Euripides. It is also possible that the name comes from the Greek "klitos" for "slope, hillside," but this seems less likely given the author's apparent interest in ancient figures (including Euripides) and the capitalization of "Clito" and other words that appear to be proper nouns in the publication where the animal was originally described.

Conocephalus conocephalus — [no common name]. This brush cricket, also known as a type of meadow katydid, can be found in southern Europe and Africa. Its scientific name comes from the Greek words "konos" and "kephale," meaning "cone head," in reference to the shape of the insect's head.

Corticea corticea — redundant skipper. This skipper is described as being mostly brown and unmarked with a grey spot on the underside of its wings. It inhabits Venezuela and Mexico. The origin of the scientific name is unclear, but it might come from the Latin word "corticeus," meaning "tree bark," in reference to its color and lack of vivid markings, perhaps giving it a tendency to resemble or blend in with tree bark.

Cossus cossus — goat moth. This large moth is found in northern Africa, Asia, and Europe, and has a wingspan up to 3.7 inches. Its scientific name appears to come from the Latin word for "woodworm," a worm or grub found in wood. The caterpillars of the goat moth feed in the trunks and branches of trees, so presumably the scientific name is a reference to goat moth caterpillars. Pliny the Elder reported in his *Historia Naturalis* that a grub called "cossus" was a considered a Roman delicacy after it was fed with flour. Some believe that this grub was the goat moth.

***Crangon crangon* — common shrimp.** This commercially important sea creature's scientific name is a Latinized form of the Greek work for shrimp, "krangon." This animal, also commonly known as the brown shrimp, is a popular food in Belgium, the Netherlands, northern Germany, and Denmark.

***Crenda crenda* — [no common name].** This skipper has medium brown wings with complex bands of light brown, dark brown, and white, and it inhabits Brazil. The origin of the scientific name is unclear, and there is little information upon which to make a reliable guess. The name might refer to a portion of the name of the locality where the type specimen was collected, as was often the case for species named by entomologist W.H. Evans, or it may reflect some other unknown whim of his. The scientific name of this species was not a tautonym and this species was classified as *Chiomara crenda* until it was reclassified in 2019.

***Cressida cressida* — big greasy butterfly.** The origin of the scientific name of this swallowtail butterfly is difficult to pin down. The word "cressida" seems to come from the Greek word "chrysos" meaning "golden," but that seems an unlikely source for the name of this butterfly since the mostly monochromatic males were given the name first. (Females are more yellowish in color and were originally thought to be a different species, *Papilio harmonia*.) "Cressida" is the name of a character from several Renaissance and Medieval re-tellings of the Trojan War. According to the myth, Cressida was a Trojan woman who was captured and taken hostage by the Greeks and fell in love with a Greek soldier. This seems like a more probable source for the butterfly's name as many butterflies were named after Greek and Roman mythological figures, and at least one other tautonymously named butterfly has a myth-inspired name—see *Ariadne ariadne*. The common name "big greasy" refers to the greasy appearance of their transparent, waxy wings. They can be found in northern Australia and New Zealand.

Cumbre cumbre — **[no common name].** This skipper is described as having wings that are brown with a greyish fringe and white spots, and it inhabits Brazil. The origin of the scientific name is unclear, and there is little information upon which to make a reliable guess. It may come from the Spanish or Portuguese word "cumbre" (or similar) for "ridge, summit." Perhaps the name refers to a ridge or summit where the first specimen of this species was obtained. The entomologist who first described it, William Schaus, appears to have drawn from Portuguese words when naming other Brazilian species, including Latinized versions of local words for natural features including "calcarea" ("limestone") and "terrens" ("land"). Many other of Schaus's names refer to the cities or countries where the species were found, including "guadala" (Guadalajara, Mexico), "paulensis" (Sao Paulo, Brazil), "grenadensis" (Grenada), "janeira" (Rio de Janeiro, Brazil), "bahiensis" (Bahia, Brazil), "jamaicensis" (Jamaica), "jamaca" (Jamaica), "coatepeca" (Coatepec, Mexico), "castrensis" (Castro, Parana, Brazil), and "friburgensis" (Nova Friburgo, Brazil). So it seems plausible that the scientific name of this species refers in some way to the locality where the type specimen was obtained.

Cynea cynea — **cynea skipper.** This skipper is described as being mostly dark brown in color with grey-white on its underside. It inhabits Venezuela, Colombia, and Mexico. The origin of the scientific name is unclear, and there is little information upon which to make a reliable guess. It may be a reference to the dog-skin cap of Greek mythology known as the "cynea" that was gifted to Hades by the Cyclops. This cap, named from the Greek words for "dog skin" or "dog hide," gave its wearer the power of invisibility. This, in turn, is the likely source of the name "Hades," from "a – eidon," meaning "unseen." Another possibility is that the skipper's name refers to the Cyanean Rocks of Greek mythology or to the ancient Lycian town of Cyaneae, but these seems less likely given the difference in spelling of "cyanea" or "cyaneae" versus "cynea."

Cyrina cyrina — [no common name]. This skipper has dark brown or black wings with several white spots, and it inhabits India, Thailand, and Brunei. The origin of the scientific name is unclear, and there is little information upon which to make a reliable guess. It might refer to the Greek mythological princess Cyrene, or to the city of northern Africa named after her. The entomologist who named it, William Chapman Hewitson, appears to have named several other species after ancient cities. Indeed, the very next species listed in Hewitson's 1876 publication is named after the ancient city of Maracanda. This species no longer has a tautonymous name and is currently classified as *Creteus cyrina*.

Danis danis — large green-banded blue. This beautify butterfly has wings that are mostly blue or black with vivid patches of white and metallic green on top, and undersides that have complex patterns of black spots within metallic blue-green patches. This species inhabits Australia and New Guinea. The scientific name appears to be a reference to the butterfly subfamily Danainae or to the tribe Danaini, because in the original description of the species, it is said that due to its appearance this species could be included among the Danaids. The taxon names Danainae and Danaini, in turn, come from Greek mythology, which was often a source of inspiration for butterfly names. In his tenth edition of *Systema Naturae*, Carl Linnaeus even provided a brief footnote explaining that his "*Danai*" taxons were named after the Danaides of Greek mythology, which were the fifty daughters of Danaus, a mythical king of Libya. According to the myth, the daughters were forced to marry the fifty sons of Aegyptus, the twin brother of Danaus. All but one of the daughters killed their husbands on their wedding night. Those daughters were condemned to spend eternity carrying water to a bottomless bathtub that could never be filled.

Decinea decinea — Huastecan skipper. This skipper is described as being dark brown in color with transparent spots and yellowish-orange marks. It inhabits Brazil, Venezuela, Peru, Paraguay, and Mexico. The origin of the scientific name is unclear, and there is little information upon which to make a reliable guess. It might relate to the Greek word "deka" for "ten." The common name refers to the La Huasteca region of Mexico.

Defectrix defectrix — **[no common name].** This Panamanian huntsman spider likely gets its scientific name from the Latin word "defectus" and the feminine suffix "-trix," meaning a female deserter, rebel, or defector. Huntsman spiders are so named because their prey is not captured in webs but is actively stalked and run-down with stealth and speed. The scientific name might allude to their behavior of "deserting" one location to chase prey, or it might be a nod to an issue of political importance to the politically active Russian entomologist who named it in 1925.

Ebusus ebusus — **ebusus skipper.** This skipper has reddish-brown coloring with one large white spot on each of the rear wigs. It is found in Suriname. The origin of the scientific name is unclear, and there is little information upon which to make a reliable guess. "Ebusus" was an early Roman name for the Spanish island of Ibiza in the Mediterranean Sea. It is unclear why this species would be given this name, but naming skippers after ancient cities was not uncommon in the 18th and 19th centuries when many lepidopterans like this one were described.

Erina erina — **small dusky-blue.** This gossamer-winged butterfly is found in Australia and Indonesia. Its wings are dark brown with a purple sheen on top, and light brown on bottom. The origin of the scientific name is unclear, but it might refer to the Furies of ancient Greek mythology. The original specific name assigned to this species was "Erinus"—an alternative spelling of "Erinyes"—the name for the Furies, and the entomologist who described this species assigned several other names from ancient mythology to butterflies in the same publication. This species no longer has a tautonymous name and is currently classified as *Candalides erinus*.

Ephippiger ephippiger — **saddle-backed bush cricket.** This cricket is common in southwestern Europe where it is used in farming to control plant-dwelling pest insects. Its scientific name comes from the Latin word "ephippium," meaning "saddle of a horse." This cricket has very small wings, which causes its prothorax to resemble a saddle.

Floricomus floricomus — **tube-nosed hairy-faced money spider.** This North American dwarf spider gets its scientific name from the Latin word meaning "crowned with flowers," likely in reference to the color or hair pattern on its dorsal side. The common name "money spider" refers to a superstition that if such a spider is running toward you, it has come to spin you new clothes and financial good fortune. This species no longer has a tautonymous name and is currently classified as *Floricomus rostratus.*

Forcipata forcipata — **[no common name].** This leafhopper is found in North America and Europe. It gets its scientific name from the Latin word "forcipatus," meaning "shaped like forceps." This refers to the male genitalia, which ends in forceps-like claspers.

Furcula furcula — **sallow kitten.** The scientific name is the Latin word for a "small, two-pronged fork," and refers to the long, forked tail of this species when it is a caterpillar. This moth has grey-white hair and can be found in Europe, Asia, and North America. It is the moths' hairiness that gives them their common name, "kittens."

Gallio gallio — **[no common name].** This skipper has medium brown wings with several small, yellowish spots, and it inhabits Brazil. The origin of the scientific name is unclear, and there is little information upon which to make a reliable guess. It might refer to ancient Roman senator Lucius Junius Gallio Annaeanus, as the entomologist who named it, Paul Mabille, would sometimes refer to ancient figures when naming new species. This species no longer has a tautonymous name and is currently classified as *Gallio carasta.*

Gesta gesta — **impostor duskywing.** This skipper is light brown or reddish-brown in color with subtle lighter brown markings. It inhabits Brazil, Argentina, Paraguay, and Cuba. The origin of the scientific name is unclear, and there is little information upon which to make a reliable guess. The

Latin word "gesta" refers to "deeds," such as in the literary compilation *Gesta Romanorum* ("Deeds of the Romans") or the chronicle of Roman history *Res Gestae* ("Things Done"). The Latin word can also be translated as "having been carried or borne," although this meaning also bears no obvious relationship to this skipper species.

Goliathus goliathus — **Goliath beetle.** This large, colorful beetle of equatorial Africa can reach up to 4.3 inches in length and is one of the largest insects on Earth. Its scientific name refers to the Biblical giant, Goliath. This species no longer has a tautonymous name and is currently classified as *Goliathus goliatus.*

Grapsus grapsus — **red rock crab.** The scientific name of this crab is derived from the Greek word "grapsaios" meaning "crab." The red rock crab is found along the Pacific coast of Mexico, Central America, and South America. It is also known as "abuete negro" and "Sally Lightfoot crab." This species was collected by Charles Darwin during his voyages on the HMS Beagle, and also by the first comprehensive study of the fauna of the Gulf of California, carried out by John Steinbeck and others. Steinbeck wrote: "Many people have spoken at length of the Sally Lightfoots. In fact, everyone who has seen them has been delighted with them. . . . They have remarkable eyes and an extremely fast reaction time. . . . They seem to be able to run in any of four directions; but more than this, perhaps because of their rapid reaction time, they appear to read the mind of their hunter. They escape the long-handled net, anticipating from what direction it is coming. If you walk slowly, they move slowly ahead of you in droves. If you hurry, they hurry. When you plunge at them, they seem to disappear in a puff of blue smoke—at any rate, they disappear. It is impossible to creep up on them. . . . Man reacts peculiarly but consistently in his relationship with Sally Lightfoot. His tendency eventually is to scream curses, to hurl himself at them, and to come up foaming with rage and bruised all over his chest. Thus, Tiny, leaping forward, slipped and fell and hurt his arm. He never forgot nor forgave his enemy. From then on he attacked Lightfoots by every foul means he could contrive and a training

in Monterey street fighting has equipped him well for this kind of battle. He
hurled rocks at them; he smashed at them with boards; and he even considered poisoning them. Eventually we did catch a few Sallys, but we think they
were the halt and the blind, the simpletons of their species. With reasonably
well-balanced and non-neurotic Lightfoots we stood no chance."

Grumicha grumicha — **[no common name].** This species of caddisfly inhabits Brazil. The origin of its scientific name is unclear, but it may refer to the
Brazilian cherry tree commonly known as grumichama, perhaps because this
species of caddisfly can be found living in the wood of these trees.

Gryllotalpa gryllotalpa — **European mole cricket.** This insect is widespread
in Europe and has been introduced to the eastern United States. The scientific
name comes from the Latin "gryllus," meaning "cricket," and "talpa," meaning "mole." This refers to the similarities that this cricket shares with moles.
They have dense fur, subterranean habits, and mole-like forelegs adapted
for digging. In this way, the mole cricket is a good example of convergent
evolution—*i.e.*, the independent evolution of similar features in species of
different periods or epochs in time.

Hilarella hilarella — **[no common name].** This flesh fly is found in North
America. The origin of its scientific name is unclear, but it may be a diminutive form of the Latin word "hilara," meaning "cheerful," in reference to its
colorful appearance as compared to similar species. Flesh flies are so named
because they deposit hatching maggots on carrion, dung, decaying material,
and open wounds of mammals.

Hottentotta hottentotta — **Congo red alligator back scorpion.** This scorpion
is found widely across Africa. The scientific name refers to the nomadic indigenous Khoekhoen people of southwestern Africa, who were known as the
"Hottentot" when this species was named. The venom of certain *Hottentotta*
species is relatively potent, and the Indian red scorpion (*Hottentotta tamulus*)
is considered the most lethal scorpion species in the world.

Idea idea — **Linnaeus's idea.** The *Idea* genus contains butterflies known as tree nymphs or paper butterflies. This species is also known as the rice paper butterfly. Carl Linnaeus is considered the father of modern taxonomy, and it was his idea of formalized binomial nomenclature for plants and animals that is still in use today. The word "idea" comes from Greek, meaning the "form" or "pattern" of a thing. In the butterfly context, "idea" refers to the patterns on their wings.

Jajinia jajinia — **[no common name].** This Venezeulan harvestman gets its scientific name from the town of Jaji in the state of Meridia, Venezuela, where the type specimen was found.

Joanna joanna — **Joanna's skipper.** This species of skipper is found in Mexico and Panama, and it has light brown wings with white spots and a brownish-grey body. The origin of the scientific name is unclear, and there is little information upon which to make a reliable guess. It might come from the proper noun "Joanna," or it might instead refer to a portion of the name of the locality where the type specimen was collected, as was often the case for species named by entomologist W.H. Evans, or it may reflect some other unknown whim of his. One possibility is that "Joanna" comes from the country name "Guiana," which is where another species in the *Joanna* genus also described by Evans was found (*Joanna boxi*).

Lamponia lamponia — **[no common name].** This skipper is described as being dark brown, pale brown, and reddish-brown in color with transparent and white spots. It inhabits Brazil. The origin of the scientific name is unclear, and there is little information upon which to make a reliable guess. It might come from the name of the ancient Greek city "Lamponeia," the Greek word "lampas" for "shine," or the name of the ancient Roman plebeian family "gens Lamponia." The most likely explanation would appear to be the Greek city "Lamponeia," as entomologist William Chapman Hewitson appears to have been fond of naming skippers after ancient towns.

Lento lento — [**no common name**]. This species is described as having red, yellow, and orange coloring, and as inhabiting Brazil. The origin of the scientific name is unclear, and there is little information upon which to make a reliable guess. It might come from the Latin word for "slow" ("lentus") or the Latin word meaning "to bend" ("lentare"). It is unclear why this species would be given this name. The entomologist who named it, Paul Mabille, appears to have described many skippers by using Latin words for their physical characteristics, including *Pamphila caerulans* for a skipper with a vivid cerulean color on its wings. Perhaps this species was observed as moving slowly. "Lento" was also the name of a Roman playwright and politician, who might have inspired the skipper's name, given that Mabille's description compares this species to another species seemingly named after Greek philosopher Epictetus, a near-contemporary of the Roman Lento.

Levina levina — [**no common name**]. This skipper is described as having a rust-yellow color with narrow stripes of brownish-red, and it inhabits Brazil. The origin of the scientific name is unclear, and there is little information upon which to make a reliable guess. There was an ancient Greek city named Levina on the island of Crete, which might be referenced in the skipper's name, but it is unclear why this name would be given. Alternatively, the name might come from the Latin word "levis," meaning "light" or "swift," perhaps in reference to the animal's size or movement, or from the proper noun "Levina" of some notable person or place.

Librita librita — **librita skipper.** This skipper is described as having brownish-red and rusty yellow markings and it inhabits Panama, Mexico, and Guatemala. The origin of the scientific name is unclear, and there is little information upon which to make a reliable guess. The name could refer to any of several different, similar words. For instance, it may refer to Libra, the constellation and myth-based astrological sign associated with justice and balance. It could also be a meaningless word or a word of personal significance to the entomologist who named it. Such arbitrary naming practices continue to this day: In 2009 a new genus was created to reclassify a species that was previously within *Librita*, and the new genus was given the name *Neposa*. The entomologists who created the new genus explained that "Neposa" is a meaningless anagram of another genus, "*Poanes*." This illustrates how difficult it can be to determine the etymological origins of scientific names when no explanations are provided by the authors of the names.

Ludens ludens — **ludens skipper.** This skipper is found in Costa Rica, Panama, and Venezuela, and it has reddish-brown wings with yellow spots. The origin of the scientific name is unclear, and there is little information upon which to make a reliable guess. It appears to be the Latin word for "playing" or "teasing" from the word "ludere." This species was described by Paul Mabille and the very next species described in his 1891 publication is given the specific name "illudens," which is Latin for "ridiculing." Both species at that time were contained in the genus *Cobalus*, which is the Latin word for "goblin," coming from the Greek word "kobalos." This results in names akin to "teasing goblin" and "mocking goblin." It appears that Mabille had some fun with these names—one skipper is a goblin making unkind jokes and the other one is playfully joining in the fun.

Majella majella — **[no common name].** This achilid planthopper can be found in Queesland, Australia. The origin of its scientific name is unclear, but it appears to refer to either the Majella massif in the Apennine Mountains, the Portuguese explorer Ferdinand Magellan, or the Latin word "major," meaning "great," with a diminutive suffix. This species no longer has a tautonymous name and is currently classified as *Deferunda majella*.

Mashuna mashuna — **Mashuna ringlet.** This butterfly is mostly dark brown and has a small black dot on each of its forewings. It is found in Zimbabwe in marshy areas of grasslands. Its scientific name refers to Mashunaland, a region in northern Zimbabwe where this species of butterfly is found.

Megacephala megacephala — **big-headed tiger beetle.** The name of this beetle means "large head" in Greek. This tiger beetle can be found in savanna-type habitats of Africa. About 400,000 species of beetle have been discovered, which is estimated to be 40% of all known animal species and 27% of all known species of life.

Melolontha melolontha — **common cockchafer.** This European beetle gets its scientific name from the Greek word "melolonthe," literally meaning "fruit destroyer," in reference to the animal's voracious appetite. The common name "cockchafer" is a combination of the 17th century word "cock," meaning "large," and the Old English word "chafer," meaning "gnawer." The common cockchafer is also known as the May bug and the doodlebug. Other species within *Melolontha* include the forest cockchafer and the large cockchafer.

Menander menander — **menander metalmark.** This beautiful butterfly has wings that are dark brown with vivid blue-green, metallic-looking marks. The undersides of the wings are almost entirely white with small brown spots. It inhabits much of South America and parts of Central America, including Brazil, Bolivia, Peru, Colombia, Suriname, Costa Rica, and French Guiana. The common name refers to the small, metallic-looking spots often found on wings of this family of butterflies. The scientific name appears to be a reference to ancient Greek dramatist Menander.

Meza meza — **common missile.** This butterfly has dark brown wings with white spots and is found in western Africa. The origin of the scientific name is unclear, and it does not have any obvious relationship to the physical characteristics of this species or its locality. In fact, all of the twenty-five species described by entomologist William Chapman Hewitson in the 1877 publication where this "meza" is described have specific names that are difficult to trace and often similar in length and letters used. These include the following species that were placed in the same genus as *meza* by Hewitson: *zema, zimra, uza, goza, meda, midia, maheta,* and *hazarma.* The name "meza" is an anagram of the species "zema," so perhaps this was the reason for the name. It is not uncommon for species names to be anagrams of other names, and the Hewitson species name *Hesperia zimra* listed here is an anagram of another Hewitson species name *Ithomia mirza.* Another possibility is that "meza" bears some etymological relationship to the word "missile," which is the common name and comes from the Latin "missilis" from "missus" for "sent off, thrown."

Misius misius — **misius skipper.** This skipper has dark brown wings with large, vivid, orange marks, and it inhabits Brazil and Peru. The origin of the scientific name is unclear, and there is little information upon which to make a reliable guess. It appears to refer to a person or place of ancient Rome or Greece, perhaps to the Misius river of the ancient Roman region of Picenum. Other skippers described by entomologist Paul Mabille in the same genus and the same publication include "Xenarchus" (1st century BC Greek philosopher) and "Meton" (5th century BC Greek mathematician), so it is plausible that he took inspiration from ancient names when naming this species. This is further supported by the fact that the first letters of these particular names are capitalized in Mabille's original descriptions, which was unusual, suggesting that these names came from proper nouns.

Moeros moeros — **[no common name].** This skipper inhabits Suriname and Trinidad and is light brown with reddish-brown patches and transparent spots. The origin of the scientific name is unclear, and there is little information upon which to make a reliable guess. It might refer to a large lake of northern Egypt, the Moeris. It might alternatively have an etymological relationship to a different, perhaps similar genus of skippers, *Moeris*. Yet another explanation is that it refers to the Greek mythological goddess of destiny, Moerae.

Molla molla — **[no common name].** This skipper has wings that are dark brown on the top and the underside, and it inhabits Brazil. The origin of the scientific name is unclear, and there is little information upon which to make a reliable guess. The name might refer to a portion of the name of the locality where the type specimen was collected, as was often the case for species named by entomologist W.H. Evans, or it may reflect some other unknown whim of his.

Mortola mortola — [**no common name**]. This camel spider is found in Argentina and it is the only member of the genus *Mortola*. It is described as having a reddish-yellow color and being approximately 14 millimeters in length. Its scientific name honors the distinguished geologist Edelmira Mortola.

Myopina myopina — [**no common name**]. This species of fly is found in central and northern Europe. Its scientific name appears to come from the Greek word "muops," meaning "horsefly."

Narcosius narcosius — [**no common name**]. This skipper is described as having mostly black wings with shiny green hair on the head, body, and middle of the wings. It inhabits Suriname. The origin of the scientific name is unclear, and there is little information upon which to make a reliable guess. It appears to come from the Greek word "narke" referring to a state of "numbness" or "sleep."

Neita neita — **Neita brown.** This species of butterfly has medium brown wings with vivid red and black marks on its forewings. It is found in grasslands and grassy savanna hillsides in South Africa. The origin of the scientific name is unclear, and there is little information upon which to make a reliable guess. It might refer to Neith, also spelled Neit, an early ancient Egyptian deity said to be the creator of the universe. Alternatively, it might refer to a person or place of significance in the locality where it was found.

Nyctelius nyctelius — **violet-banded skipper.** This butterfly is found in North, Central, and South America. Its name comes from Greek and means "of the night." The scientific name is also a nickname given to the Greek god Dionysus because his festivals were celebrated at night.

Orthos orthos — **orthos skipper.** This species of skipper inhabits Panama, Trinidad, Brazil, and Peru, and has light brown wings with two small white spots on each wing. The origin of the scientific name is unclear, and there is little information upon which to make a reliable guess. It appears to come from the Greek prefix "ortho-," meaning "straight." Alternatively, it may refer to a proper noun of ancient Greece as is the case for many butterfly, skipper, and moth names. Orthos was an ancient city-state in Thessaly and was also the name of a two-headed guard dog in ancient Greek mythology. The two-headed dog seems to be the most plausible source, given the trend of using ancient mythology for lepidopteran names. For instance, the entomologist who named this species also named another species "achelous," seemingly after a Greek mythological river god of the same name.

Pamba pamba — [**no common name**]. This skipper has medium brown wings with a large white marking on top of each of its hindwings, and it inhabits Ecuador. The scientific name appears to be based on the latter part of the locality name "Balzapamba," which is an area in Ecuador where the specimen described by entomologist W.H. Evans was found. Evans appears to have referred to the locality names of type specimens often when naming new species, including by using only a portion of the locality name, as was done for the Guatemalan skipper *Cogia mala* and other tautonymously named lepidopterans. In fact, the type locality of the only other species in this genus, *Pamba boyaca*, is the town of Arcabuco in the Department of Boyaca in Colombia.

Passova passova — **passova firetip.** This skipper is described as being greenish-black with scarlet red markings and a white underside. It inhabits the Amazon River area including Colombia, Peru, Brazil, and Guyana. The vivid red marks on the tips of its head, abdomen, and wings are why it is commonly known as a "firetip." The origin of the scientific name is unclear, and there is little information upon which to make a reliable guess. It might come from a Greek or Latin root word for "sprinkle" ("passein") or "pace" ("passus"). Another possibility is that the name refers to some ancient location, as it appears that the entomologist who first assigned the name, William Chapman Hewitson, was fond of using ancient city names for skipper names. In the same publication where we find Hewitson's description of this "passova" species, we also see species in the same genus apparently named for the ancient towns of "Gortyna," "Pedaia," "Hadassa" (Hadasha), and "Zereda," among others. Whatever the case, it is unclear why this species would be given this name.

Pastria pastria — **[no common name].** This skipper has wings that are medium brown with light and dark brown markings, and it inhabits New Guinea. The origin of the scientific name is unclear, and there is little information upon which to make a reliable guess. The name might refer to a portion of the name of the locality where the type specimen was collected, as was often the case for species named by entomologist W.H. Evans, or it may reflect some other unknown whim of his. Alternatively, it might refer to the Greek word "pastos," meaning "sprinkled with salt," perhaps in reference to the light-colored markings on this skipper's wings.

Phalanta phalanta — **common leopard butterfly.** This orange and black butterfly is also known as the spotted rustic. It is found in sub-Saharan Africa and southern Asia. The origin of the scientific name is unclear, and there is little information upon which to make a reliable guess. One possibility is that it comes from the Sanskrit word "phalanta," meaning "fruitful," although it is not clear why such a name would be given to this species. This species no longer has a tautonymous name and is currently classified as *Phalanta phalantha*. The creation of the tautonym appears to be the result of a misspelling.

Pilosa pilosa — **[no common name].** This harvestman species is in the Zalmoxidae family, named after the Thracian god Zalmoxis. It is found in northern Venezuela and its scientific name is the Spanish word for "hairy," in reference to the dense hair that covers most of its body.

Plumbago plumbago — **[no common name].** This skipper is described as being brown with faint grey spots, and it inhabits Brazil. The origin of the scientific name is unclear, and there is little information upon which to make a reliable guess. The word in Latin refers to a "type of lead ore," from "plumbum" for "lead." The word is also the name of a genus of flowering plants native to warm temperate and tropical regions, including Brazil. The plant's name likely comes from the lead-blue color of its flowers, the ability of the sap to create lead-colored stains, or Pliny the Elder's belief that the plant was a cure for lead poisoning. The skipper's name might be a reference to the fact that the skipper can be found where a species of plumbago plant grows.

Pollicipes pollicipes — **Atlantic goose barnacle.** This barnacle found in the northern Atlantic Ocean appears to get its name from the Latin words "pollicis," meaning "thumb," and "pedis," meaning "foot," perhaps in reference to the shape of its foot. The common name goose barnacle resulted from a belief that barnacle geese were born from this crustacean through spontaneous generation. The confusion was prompted by the facts that barnacle geese were never seen nesting in Europe, people did not yet know that birds migrate, and the two species have similarities in color. Needless to say, there is no evidence to support the claim that birds spontaneously hatch out of barnacles.

Polyctor polyctor — **polyctor tufted-skipper.** This skipper is described as having milky white wings with greenish-brown marks and white spots. It inhabits areas from Argentina and Brazil north to Costa Rica. The scientific name appears to refer to one of several Greek mythological figures including a Polyctor who was an Egyptian prince slain on his wedding night by his wife, a Polyctor who made a basin of stone in Ithaca, or a Polyctor referenced in Homer's *Iliad* as the supposed father of Hermes. Interestingly, the species name appears to have been misspelled as "polyotor" in the first publication where this species was described. This misspelling has since been corrected, but it illustrates another challenge to determining scientific name origins when etymological explanations are not provided in the original species descriptions.

Polyspila polyspila — **leopard ladybug.** This leaf beetle is found in Brazil, and it has bright yellow forewings with several black spots on each. Its scientific name comes from the Greek words "polys," meaning "many," and "spilos," meaning "spot," in reference to this spotted pattern. This species no longer has a tautonymous name and is currently classified as *Calligrapha polyspila*.

Pompeius pompeius — **pompeius skipper.** This skipper is mostly light brown with dark brown and black markings. It inhabits Brazil, Mexico, and Argentina. The scientific name appears to refer to the ancient Roman general Gnaeus Pompeius Magnus, or to the ancient city Pompeii that was buried in volcanic ash in the eruption of Mount Vesuvius in 79 AD.

Potimirim potimirim — **potimirim shrimp.** This small shrimp inhabits freshwaters of Brazil. Its scientific name comes from the Tupi words "poti" for "shrimp," and "mirim" for "little."

Pratorum pratorum — **[no common name].** Whether this scientific name was ever assigned to a species is unclear. There appear to be no scientific sources that recognize *Pratorum pratorum* as a current or former animal name. Assuming this animal exists within *Pratorum*, it is a chironomid fly, or "nonbiting midge," and it inhabits northern Europe. Its name appears to come from the Latin word "pratum," meaning "meadow," perhaps because this species can be found in meadows. This name might refer to what was formerly known as *Camptocladius pratorum*, which is currently classified as *Smittia pratorum*. Accordingly, it no longer has a tautonymous name.

Propertius propertius — **propertius skipper.** This skipper inhabits Peru, Paraguay, Brazil, and Argentina, and it has a dark reddish color with large white markings on its wings. The scientific name appears to be a reference to Sextus Propertius, a Latin elegiac poet of the 1st century BC. The entomologist who described this species, Johan Christian Fabricius, used ancient names when describing other species. In fact, in the publication in which he describes this species, the very next species is named after Albius Tibullus, another Latin elegiac poet and contemporary of Propertius.

Protesilaus protesilaus — **great kite-swallowtail.** Carl Linnaeus is credited with naming over 11,000 organisms, including 192 butterflies and moths. For some reason, Linnaeus decided to name the butterflies and a few moths he thought were butterflies after people and places in ancient mythology.

Protesilaus is one such name, and it refers to a Greek suitor of Helen who was the first to step ashore and the first to die in the Trojan War.

Punta punta — **[no common name].** This skipper has wings that are dark brown with a few white spots, and it inhabits Brazil. The origin of the scientific name is unclear, and there is little information upon which to make a reliable guess. The name might refer to a portion of the name of the locality where the type specimen was collected, as was often the case for species named by entomologist W.H. Evans, or it may reflect some other unknown whim of his.

Pyrrhyllis pyrrhyllis — **[no common name].** This achilid planthopper can be found in Queensland, Australia. The origin of its scientific name is unclear, but it appears to come from the Greek word "purrhos," meaning "flame-colored," with a diminutive suffix. The name might refer to the planthopper's color, which was originally described as being yellowish and "smoky" black.

Racta racta — **racta skipper.** This skipper has dark brown wings with vivid, reddish-brown and yellow markings, and it inhabits Peru. The origin of the scientific name is unclear, and there is little information upon which to make a reliable guess. The name might refer to a portion of the name of the locality where the type specimen was collected, as was often the case for species named by entomologist W.H. Evans, or it may reflect some other unknown whim of his. For instance, the name might refer to the small Peruvian town of Raccaraccay, which is near to the area of Uruhuasi where the type specimen was found, although there is little to suggest that W.H. Evans was aware of this small town.

Ranina ranina — **red frog crab.** This crab, also known as the spanner crab, is found throughout tropical and subtropical habitats. The scientific name comes from the Latin word "rana," meaning "frog." These crabs are so named because of their frog-like appearance.

Repens repens — **[no common name].** This skipper has wings that are medium brown with faint white spots, and it inhabits Brazil. The origin of the scientific name is unclear, and there is little information upon which to make a reliable guess. The name might refer to a portion of the name of the locality where the type specimen was collected, as was often the case for species named by entomologist W.H. Evans, or it may reflect some other unknown whim of his. For instance, the word "repens" is the Latin word for "sudden, unexpected" and is also the Latin word for "crawling, creeping." Perhaps the name refers to the skipper's habit of "suddenly" appearing, or to some "creeping" behavior. Or perhaps the name refers to the fact that the skipper can be found in one of several plant species also named "repens," such as *Arachis repens*. Still another possibility is that the name could be derivative of the Latin word "ripensis," meaning "of a riverbank," in reference to the fact that the type specimen was collected from the Capivari River in Brazil.

Ridens ridens — **frosted skipper.** This skipper is described as having dark brown and black wings with white markings and black spots, and as inhabiting the Chiriqui province of Panama. The origin of the scientific name is unclear, and there is little information upon which to make a reliable guess. It may be a reference to the Latin word "rideo" for "laughing, ridiculing," or may have been inspired by the notion of a "Homo ridens," a view introduced by Aristotle that humans are the only animals that laugh. Another possibility is that the name was inspired by "Erycina ridens," an epithet for the Roman god Venus.

Roche roche — **[no common name].** This spider is found only in the Seychelles and is currently considered vulnerable to extinction. It is a member of the six-eyed spider family, Ochyroceratidae. This spider's scientific name refers to the Roche Caiman Bird Sanctuary on the island of Mahe, which is the type locality where this species was found. It is the only species in the genus *Roche*.

Sabina sabina — [no common name]. This skipper has dark brown wings with a few transparent spots and a mostly white underside. It inhabits Brazil. The scientific name appears to refer to the ancient Sabine people of the Apennine Mountains or to the Sabine Hills that they inhabited. Other species names that refer to ancient people or places by this entomologist in the same publication where "Sabina" is described include "Lucretius" (Roman poet), "Lapithes" (son of Apollo), and "Ittona" (epithet of Athena). This species no longer has a tautonymous name and is currently classified as *Saniba sabina*. It was discovered in 2003 that the generic name *Sabina* was already in use for a type of bristle worm, so the generic name of this skipper was changed to the anagram "Saniba."

Sacrator sacrator — [no common name]. This species of skipper is described as having wings that are mostly dark brown on top and brown with a broad yellow band on the underside. It inhabits Colombia. The origin of the scientific name is unclear, but it appears to be the Latin word for "priest, consecrator." As with so many lepidopteran names, it is unclear why this species would be given this name.

Salatis salatis — variable scarlet-eye skipper. This skipper is found in Suriname, Colombia, and Brazil, and is described as being a greenish and yellow-brown color with small white spots. The origin of the scientific name is unclear, and there is little information upon which to make a reliable guess. It may refer to Salatis, the first Hyksos king who ruled Lower Egypt in around 1650 BC. Other species described by the entomologist who described this one, Caspar Stoll, and that appear in the same genus and the same publication have names of ancient Egyptian rulers including Egyptian pharaohs Menes and Nitocris.

Saturnus saturnus — [no common name]. This skipper has light brown wings with white spots and inhabits Brazil and French Guiana. The scientific name is the Latin name for the Roman mythological god Saturn. The entomologist who described this species gave mythological names to several others, including *phineus* (king of Thrace), *helius* (god of the sun), *metis* (goddess and oceanid nymph), *orion* (giant huntsman), *proteus* (sea god), and others.

Scalpellum scalpellum — **velvet goose barnacle.** This small goose barnacle can be found in the eastern Atlantic Ocean. The scientific name appears to be the Latin word for scalpel, which comes from "scalpere" for "to scratch, carve." This might be in reference to the sharpness of this barnacle's shell.

Scolytus scolytus — **large elm bark beetle.** This 3.5 – to 6-millimeter-long bark beetle is a major vector of Dutch elm disease, which rapidly kills elm trees in Eurasia. Other *Scolytus* species are responsible for spreading the disease in North America. All bark beetles are members of the Scolytidae family, the name of which comes from the Greek word for "to strip" or "to cut short." The name is likely in reference to the manner in which these beetles feed on the inner bark of trees, often leading to the death of the tree.

Serianus serianus — **[no common name].** This arachnid belongs to an order known commonly as pseudoscorpions or false scorpions. They are very small and flat with pear-shaped bodies. They have pincer-like appendages that resemble those of scorpions, and they also spin silk from glands in their jaws to make cocoons for mating, molting, or waiting out cold weather. This species is only 2.5 millimeters long and inhabits dry areas of North America. The scientific name appears to come from the Greek word "ser," meaning "silk," and the Latin suffix "-anus," meaning "pertaining to," in reference to the animal's silk cocoons. One of the specimens used when describing this new species was found in a silk nest on a beach. Alternatively, the name might come from the Latin word "sertum" for "joined," in reference to its distinctive, segmented legs.

Sodreana sodreana — **[no common name].** This species of harvestman is a member of the Gonyleptidae family, named from the Greek words "gony" for "knee," and "leptos" for "thin." It is found in Brazlilian rainforests and was named after the individual who collected the first specimen to be described, Altino de Azevedo Sodre.

Speculum speculum — **hidden mirror skipper.** This skipper found in the Rondonia region of Brazil has wings that are mostly brown but have shiny grey areas on the forewings. The scientific name is a Latin word meaning "mirror" in reference to the shiny area on its wings.

Sucova sucova — **sucova skipper.** This skipper is described as having dark brown wings with blackish coloring underneath and a few whitish hairs. It inhabits the Petropolis area of Brazil, and also Paraguay. The origin of the scientific name is unclear, and there is little information upon which to make a reliable guess. It may ultimately come from the Latin word "sucus" (or the Portuguese "suco") for "juice," but it is unclear why this species would be given this name.

Therezopolis therezopolis — **[no common name].** This harvestman inhabits Brazil. Its scientific name comes from the Brazilian city of Teresopolis, which is where the type specimen of this species was found. This species no longer has a tautonymous name and is currently classified as *Graphinotus therezopolis*.

Tiacellia tiacellia — **[no common name].** This skipper is mostly brown and unmarked except for an indigo blue spot with white bands on its underside. It inhabits the Aru Islands. The origin of the scientific name is unclear, and there is little information upon which to make a reliable guess. For instance, it might refer to a local vernacular name for this species, or to some person or place of significance in the locality where the type specimen was found.

Tibicen tibicen — **morning cicada.** This cicada, also known as the swamp cicada, is widespread across much of the eastern and central United States and parts of southeastern Canada. Its scientific name is the Latin word for "piper" or "flautist," presumably in reference to this cicada's calls. It is particularly active and audible in the morning, hence its common name. This species no longer has a tautonymous name and is currently classified as *Neotibicen tibicen*.

Tosta tosta — **[no common name].** This skipper is mostly dark brown with subtle light brown bands, and it inhabits Peru and Columbia. The scientific name bears some resemblance to the Latin word "tostus" for "burned, parched," possibly in reference to its color. A more likely explanation, however, is that the scientific name is based on the latter part of the name "Iquitos," which is the Peruvian city where the specimen described by entomologist W.H. Evans was found. As seen in other species, Evans often used the locality names where type specimens were collected when naming new species. In this case, "tosta" would come from the "-tos" in "Iquitos."

Tromba tromba — **[no common name].** This skipper has medium brown wings with darker brown markings, and it inhabits Peru. The origin of the scientific name is unclear, and there is little information upon which to make a reliable guess. The name might refer to a portion of the name of the locality where the type specimen was collected, as was often the case for species named by entomologist W.H. Evans, or it may reflect some other unknown whim of his. For instance, the Spanish word "tromba" means "trumpet" or "tornado, waterspout," but it is unclear why any of these would be chosen as a name for this species.

Turmada turmada — **[no common name].** This skipper is described as having wings that are dark brown on top and light brown with olive green highlights on bottom, and it inhabits Ecuador. The origin of the scientific name is unclear, and there is little information upon which to make a reliable guess. It may come from the Latin word "turma" for a "troop of cavalry," or the Spanish word "turma" referring to a kind of potato or to a testicle, but it is unclear why such a name would be given to this species.

Valeria valeria — **common wanderer.** This beautiful butterfly, also known as the Malayan wanderer, is found in India and southeastern Asia. Its wings are pale blue and black on top, and whitish blue on bottom. Its scientific name appears to refer to the prominent ancient Roman family, gens Valeria, or to an ancient Roman city of the same name. Other ancient references in butterfly names by this same entomologist in the same publication where this species appears include "Tiresias" (blind Theban seer), "Danae" (mother of Perseus), and "Cerbera" (referring to the three-headed dog of the underworld named Cerberus). The word "valeria" is also Latin for a kind of eagle, but this seems less likely as a source for this butterfly's name given the common practice of naming butterflies for ancient people, places, and myths. This species no longer has a tautonymous name and is currently classified as *Pareronia valeria*.

Vermileo vermileo — [**no common name**]. This unusual fly-like species gets its scientific name from the Latin words "vermis" for "worm," and "leo" for "lion." Most wormlions are found in the dry regions of western Africa, but they are found on other continents as well. The name appears to refer to the way in which the larvae feed. The larvae, which look like worms, dig cone-shaped pits and sit camouflaged at the base of them, waiting for prey to unwittingly fall into the pit. The name "lion" may suggest that these animals are successful predators, given that other insects are a large portion of their diet.

Vidius vidius — [**no common name**]. This skipper is described as having a generally blackish color, although images of this species appear more medium brown than black. It inhabits the Brazilian state of Rio Grande do Sul. The origin of the scientific name is unclear, and there is little information upon which to make a reliable guess. It appears to come from the Latin word "videre," meaning "to see." This might be in reference to the skipper's physical appearance, as the original description of this species indicates that it has a blackish spot on its lower wings that, when seen from another angle, appears as two lilac-grey bands.

Xanthostigma xanthostigma — [**no common name**]. This predatory snake-fly is found in Europe and is an important predator of aphids and mites. Its scientific name appears to come from the Greek words "xanthos" for "yellow," and "stigma" for "mark," in reference to the yellow markings on its dark abdomen.

Ypiranga ypiranga — **[no common name].** This harvestman is found in Brazil, and its scientific name refers to the Ipiranga River where its type specimen was found. This river—now a brook—is located in the state of Sao Paulo and is mentioned in the country's national anthem. This species no longer has a tautonymous name and is currently classified as *Uropachylus ypiranga*.

Zera zera — **zera skipper.** This skipper is described as having greyish-brown wings with large, pale blue spots underneath. It inhabits Brazil, Venezuela, Panama, and Bolivia. The origin of the scientific name is unclear, and there is little information upon which to make a reliable guess. The name could refer to any of several different, similar words in ancient and modern languages. For instance, the Hebrew word "zera" means "seed," but it is unclear why this species would be given this name. The specific name starts with a capital letter in the publication where it was first described, while other specific names do not. This suggests that the word refers to a proper noun of significance to the entomologist who created the name, such as the name of the area of Venezuela where the species was found.

Zingha zingha — **shining red charaxes.** There is little information on whether a species ever held a valid tautonymous name of *Zingha zingha*. The taxon "zingha" first appears in the 1780 description of *Papilio zingha* by Caspar Stoll. This same species was later classified as *Charaxes zingha* in 1900. The 1900 publication lists ten synonyms of this species, none of which are tautonyms, and the binomial *Charaxes zingha* remains valid to this day. There is a 1939 publication in which a genus *Zingha* is proposed and the scientific name *Zingha zingha* is given to *Papilio zingha*, but this publication does not seem to address the 1900 description and classification of *Charaxes zingha*. In any event, this species of coastal butterfly of western Africa has wings that are black with bright orange-red patches and a colorful underside with grey, yellow, pink, and red. The origin of the scientific name is unclear, and there is little information upon which to make a reliable guess. The scientific name might be a vernacular name for the species in the locality where it was found, or it may refer to something of local significance. For instance, a 17th century queen of the Ambundu kingdoms located in what is now Angola was named Nzingha Mbande and may have been the inspiration for the name of this beautiful butterfly.

Zoma zoma — **Seychelles ray spider.** This species was first described in 1996 and is endemic to Silhouette Island of the Republic of Seychelles. The scientific name is Greek for "belt" and refers to the belt of silvery corpuscles on the spider's abdomen. As a ray spider, it constructs cone-shaped webs.

Zonia zonia — **zonia skipper.** This beautiful skipper has metallic blue, white, and black bands on its wings, and it inhabits Brazil and Panama. The scientific name refers to the Brazilian state of Amazonas, which is where the type specimen described by entomologist W.H. Evans was found.

Zygoneura zygoneura — **[no common name].** This species of dark-winged fungus gnat gets its scientific name from the Greek words "zygos," meaning "joining" or "a yoke," and "neuron," meaning "nerve, vein," and refers to the forked vein in the center of its wings. Dark-winged fungus gnats occur in many parts of the world, especially in the tropics, including in parts of Europe, Asia, and the Americas.

PART VIII:

MOLLUSKS

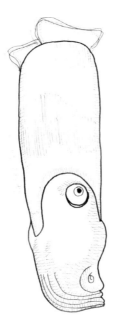

Spirula spirula

MOLLUSKS ARE INVERTEBRATE ANIMALS USUALLY found in marine and fresh-water environments and generally characterized by having a mantle with a significant cavity used for breathing, a soft body divisible into three regions (head, visceral mass, and muscular foot), and a nervous system. Over 50 of the tautonyms on this list come from names created by malacologist Felix-Pierre Jousseaume. As explained in the description of *Extra extra*, his names and classifications were not always agreed upon by his contemporaries, and many of his tautonymous names are no longer considered valid.

Achatina achatina — **Giant Ghana African snail.** This mollusk, also known as the Giant African snail, giant tiger land snail, and gigantocochlea, is a very large, terrestrial snail. Some have been measured at over 1 foot long. Its scientific name comes from the Greek word "achates," meaning "agate," which is a colorful semi-precious stone. The name might be in reference to the snail's colorful, striped shell.

Adusta adusta — **chocolate beauty.** This species of sea snail is usually 1 to 2 inches in length and has a shell that is shiny, smooth, and dark brown. It occurs in the Indian Ocean along eastern Africa. Its scientific name comes from the Latin word "adustus," meaning "burnt" or "browned," in reference to its appearance. This species no longer has a tautonymous name and is currently classified as *Erronea adusta*.

Agagus agagus — **[no common name].** The origin of this top snail's scientific name is unclear. It might come from the Greek work "agogos," meaning "leading," but it is not clear why this snail would get such a name. Alternatively, it might come from a local vernacular name for this snail, from a version of the name of the Gulf of Tadjoura where the type specimen was found, or from the Aga Mountain in Djibouti. "Top snails" are so named because their shells often resemble toy spinning tops.

Allo allo— **[no common name].** This sea snail can be found in Djibouti. The origin of its scientific name is unclear. It may refer to the Alloum River in Djibouti, to the Greek word "allos" for "different," or even to the French word for "hello." This species no longer has a tautonymous name and is currently classified as *Taranis allo*.

Anatina anatina — **smooth duck clam.** This bivalve is found in North America in the western Atlantic Ocean. Its scientific name comes from the

Latin word "anatinus," meaning "resembling a duck," in reference to its shell's resemblance to a duck bill.

Arabica arabica — **Arabian cowry.** This sea snail is found in the Indo-West Pacific from eastern and southern Africa to eastern Polynesia. Its shell has a shiny surface and a dense, irregular pattern of thin brown lines interrupted by empty spaces of cream and grey coloring. Its scientific name comes from the Latin word for "Arabic" and refers to the animal's shell pattern, which was considered similar in appearance to Arabic script. This species no longer has a tautonymous name and is currently classified as *Mauritia arabica.*

Arcinella arcinella — **Caribbean spiny jewel box.** The scientific name for this mollusk comes from the Latin word "arcanus," meaning "box," and the diminutive suffix "-ella." So-called "jewel box clams" have two-part hinged shells—a box-shaped part and a lid-shaped part—that protect their invertebrate insides.

Arcuatula arcuatula — **Arcuate mussel.** This mussel is found in the Indo-West Pacific, but its exact distribution is unknown due to confusion with similar species. Its scientific name comes from the Latin word "arcuatus," meaning "arched," in reference to the strongly arched shape of the shell, which was originally described as having a sickle-shaped contour.

Aulica aulica — **Princely volute.** This sea snail, also known as the courtier volute, inhabits the Sulu Sea of the southern Philippines. The color pattern on their shells varies from reddish-orange to whitish-brown with zig-zag markings. The scientific name comes from the Latin word "aulicus" for "princely." This might be in reference to the crown-like shape of its shell. This species no longer has a tautonymous name and is currently classified as *Cymbiola aulica.*

Bahiensis bahiensis — **[no common name].** This neotropical land snail has a long, white, and smooth shell. Its scientific name refers to the Brazillian state of Bahia, where it is found.

Barbatiella barbatiella — **[no common name]**. This bivalve mollusk is found in the Indo-Pacific Ocean. The origin of its scientific name is unclear, but it appears that this species was understood to be a smaller version of mollusks in the *Barbatia* genus, so it was given a diminutive version of that name. This species no longer has a tautonymous name and is currently classified as *Sheldonella lateralis*.

Beckianum beckianum — **[no common name]**. This land snail is native to the Caribbean Basin and can be found in Venezuela and Central America. The origin of the scientific name is unclear, but it may refer to 19th century conchologist Henrik Beck.

Bellamya bellamya — **[no common name]**. This large freshwater snail is found in Senegal. Its scientific name refers to the individual who obtained six specimens of this species for study, a Dr. Bellamy. Malacologist Felix-Pierre Jousseaume assigned the name and explained, "May this token of gratitude urge our selfless colleague to continue with perseverance the research begun with so much success." This species no longer has a tautonymous name and is currently classified as *Bellamya unicolor*.

Bertinia bertinia — **[no common name]**. This sea snail lives on rocky shores in the intertidal zone along the northwestern coasts of the Pacific Ocean. The origin of its scientific name is unclear, but it appears to honor malacologist Victor Bertin. This species no longer has a tautonymous name and is currently classified as *Cellana nigrolineata*.

Belonimorphis belonimorphis — **[no common name]**. This slender mollusk gets its name from the Greek words meaning "needle-shaped," in reference to its long, thin, tapering shell.

Bonnanius bonnanius — **[no common name]**. This tropical air-breathing land snail is found in the Fernando de Noronha archipelago in the Atlantic Ocean off Brazil. Its scientific name honors conchologist Filippo Bonanni.

This species no longer has a tautonymous name and is currently classified as *Hyperaulax ramagei.*

Bullata bullata **— [no common name].** This sea snail is found in the tropical western Atlantic Ocean. Its yellowish-orange shell is smooth and relatively large at up to 98 millimeters. The origin of its scientific name is unclear but appears to come from the Latin word "bullatus," meaning "inflated" or "bubble-like," potentially in reference to the shape of its shell.

Calcarata calcarata **— [no common name].** This species of sea snail has a shell that is a pale red color with white stripes. It might be extinct, and the specimen used to describe it is fossilized. Its scientific name comes from the Latin word "calcaratus," meaning "spurred," in reference to thorns on the side of its shell.

Clathrus clathrus **— common wentletrap.** This predatory sea snail is common along the eastern Atlantic coast in Europe. Its scientific name appears to come from the Greek word "klaithra," meaning "lattice," in reference to the intricate, lattice-like architecture and appearance of its shell. This species no longer has a tautonymous name and is currently classified as *Epitonium clathrus.*

Clypeomorus clypeomorus **— [no common name].** This sea snail is found in the Indo-Pacific from the Red Sea to the Samoa Islands. Its scientific name appears to come from the Latin words "clypeus," meaning "round shield," and "morus," meaning "mulberry tree," presumably in reference to the shape and color of its shell. This species no longer has a tautonymous name and is currently classified as *Clypeomorus bifasciata.*

Columella columella **— toothless columella snail.** This minute air-breathing land snail of eastern Europe gets its name from the Latin word for "small column," in reference to the cylindrical shape of this snail's shell.

Concholepas concholepas **— Chilean abalone.** This large sea snail's name is a combination of the Latin words "concha," meaning "shellfish," and "lepas," meaning "limpet" (which is another mollusk). Despite its common name, this animal is not actually a type of abalone but is a member of the Muricidae family, also known as the rock snails. The species is native to the coasts of Chile and Peru, where it is called "loco."

Coralliophaga coralliophaga — **coral clam.** This clam inhabits the Caribbean Sea and the Indo-Pacific. It gets its scientific name from the Greek words "korallion" for "coral," and "phagein" for "to eat."

Crassilabrum crassilabrum — **[no common name].** This sea snail is a member of the rock snail group and is found in the oceans off Chile. Its scientific name appears to come from the Latin words "crassus" and "labrum," meaning "plump lip," in reference to the shell of this animal, which has a wide, white outer lip.

Cribraria cribraria — **tan and white cowry.** This sea snail, also known as the sieve cowry, is one of the most recognizable cowries with its pale brown spots on an otherwise orange-red shell. It is found in the Red Sea and the Indian Ocean. Its scientific name comes from the Latin word "cribrum" meaning "sieve," in reference to the sieve-like pattern on its shell. This species no longer has a tautonymous name and is currently classified as *Cribrarula cribraria*.

Cumella cumella — **[no common name].** This sea snail is found in the Philippines. Its scientific name is a diminutive version of the word "Cuma," which is the name of a similar genus of sea snails to which this species was compared in its original description. This species no longer has a tautonymous name and is currently classified as *Lataxiena cumella*.

Cymbiola cymbiola — **crown volute.** This large, predatory sea snail of southeastern Asia appears to get its name from the Latin word "cymbium" for a drinking vessel shaped like a small "cymba" boat. This name may refer to the shape of the snail's shell. A closely related mollusk that also has a tautonymous name is *Cymbium cymbium*.

Cymbium cymbium — **false elephant's snout volute.** This sea snail gets its scientific name from the Latin word "cymbium," meaning "small cup." Its common name comes from the fact that it tends to be mistaken for *Cymbium glans*, the so-called elephant's snout volute. Both of these snails have long shells that may be likened to elephant trunks.

Diabolica diabolica — **[no common name].** This nucinellid mollusk of the Red Sea gets its name from the Greek word "diabolikos," generally meaning "slanderer" and later referring specifically to the Devil. It is unclear why the species has this name. The biologist who named it also created the amusing tautonymous name *Extra extra*. This species no longer has a tautonymous name and is currently classified as *Huxleyia diabolica*.

Djeddilia djeddilia — **[no common name].** This small sea snail inhabits the waters of the Mediterranean Sea, the Red Sea, and the Indian Ocean. Its scientific name refers to the Saudi Arabian city of Jeddah where the type specimen was found. This species no longer has a tautonymous name and is currently classified as *Cerithideopsilla conica*.

Dolabrifera dolabrifera — **[no common name].** This species of sea hare appears to get its scientific name from the Latin words "dolabra" for "axe head," and "ferre" for "to bear" or "to carry." It is not clear why the animal was given this name. Its body is fairly flat, so perhaps it was thought to resemble an axe.

Ensis ensis — **razor clam.** The razor clam, also known as the sword clam, gets its scientific name from the Latin word for "sword." The mollusk's shell is long, narrow, and parallel-sided, resembling a straight razor.

Exotica exotica — **[no common name].** This tellins bivalve has been found in the Red Sea. Its scientific name refers to the word "exotic," from the Greek word "exotikos," but it is unclear why this name would be given. This species no longer has a tautonymous name and is currently classified as *Exotica triradiata*.

Extra extra — **minute white sea snail.** This small sea snail appears to get its name from either the Latin word meaning "outside," or the adverb meaning "beyond the usual size or extent." It is not clear why this name was given and there is little information upon which to make a reliable guess. This name, and many others by malacologist Felix-Pierre Jousseaume, were criticized in their day for failing to follow naming customs of the time. One critic complained, "To name a shell 'Extra extra' is trifling with his fellow-workers." Another wrote that the name "should be disallowed as offending all the canons of the laws of nomenclature." It would appear that a good deal of the disapproval toward Jousseaume's names came from the belief that the species he described were not, in fact, new to science or were being poorly described. One critic explained, "The differences cited by Jousseaume, and which led him to separate, are due to inaccurate observation, and if not, they are immaterial." Another wrote that Jousseaume "has undoubtedly not yet studied the Linnean rules, or has not heard a lecture about them." This species no longer has a tautonymous name and is currently classified as *Marginella extra*. The margin shell snails are likely so named because the outer lip, or "margin," of their shells is unusually thick.

Faurotis faurotis — **Faurot's bonnet.** This large sea snail inhabits the Gulf of Aden, and its scientific name refers to the name of Lionel Faurot, the person who collected this and many other mollusk specimens for study. This species no longer has a tautonymous name and is currently classified as *Semicassis faurotis*.

Faustina faustina — **lucky arianta.** This land snail occurs in Ukraine. The origin of its scientific name is unclear, and it could come from any of several different sources. For instance, it might refer to the Faust character of German legend, to the ancient figure Faustina the Younger, or to the Latin word "faustus" for "fortunate."

Ficus ficus — **paper fig shell.** The scientific name of this sea snail comes from the Latin word for "fig." The shells of the snails in the family Ficidae are shaped somewhat like figs.

Fragum fragum — **white strawberry cockle.** The scientific name "fragum" is the Latin word for "strawberry," in reference to this mollusk's colorful, white and red shell. Cockles in the genus *Fragum* live buried in sand, extending their siphons to the surface to feed and breathe.

Fulgida fulgida — **[no common name].** This mussel is found in the Indo-West Pacific. Its scientific name is the Latin word for "shining," in reference to its shell, which is described as having a shiny appearance and a swollen, chestnut shape. This species no longer has a tautonymous name and is currently classified as *Lioberus ligneus*.

Gari gari — **truncate sunset clam.** This species of sunset shell occurs in the Indo-West Pacific. The origin of its scientific name is unclear, and there is little information upon which to make a reliable guess. For instance, it might refer to the Latin word "garum" for a fish sauce, but it is not clear why such a reference would be made in this clam's name. This species no longer has a tautonymous name and is currently classified as *Gari truncata*.

Gemma gemma — **amethyst gem clam.** The scientific name for this small saltwater clam comes from the Latin word for "gem." The shell color is whitish, with purple on both the outer and inner surfaces, hence the common name.

Gibberulus gibberulus — **humpbacked conch.** The scientific name comes from the Latin word "gibber," meaning "hump" or "humpbacked," and the diminutive suffix "-ulus." This and the common name are likely in reference to the shape of the sea snail's shell.

Glycymeris glycymeris — **dog cockle.** This marine clam, also known as the European bittersweet, gets its scientific name from the Greek word "glyky-maris," likely meaning "sweet part" (from "glykys" for "sweet" and "meris" for "part"). Its common name in French and Spanish means "sea almond," apparently in reference to its sweet, almond-like flavor.

Harpa harpa — **true harp.** This large, predatory sea snail gets its scientific name from the Latin word for "harp," likely in reference to the distinctive axial ribs protruding from its shell.

Haustellum haustellum — **Snipe's bill murex.** This sea snail belongs to the Muricidae family, commonly known as the rock snail family. Its scientific name is a diminutive form of the Latin word "haustrum," meaning a "scoop on a waterwheel." This word comes from the Latin "haurire," meaning "to drink." The word "haustellum" in English refers to a proboscis (as of an insect) used to suck blood or juices of plants. The sea snail's shell has a long and thin siphonal canal, resembling the haustellum of an insect.

Hippopus hippopus — **horse's hoof clam.** This mollusk is a member of the giant clam subfamily and is also known as the bear paw clam and the strawberry clam. Its scientific name comes from the Greek words for "horse" and "foot," apparently in reference to the fact that this large clam looks like a horse's hoof. The Greek word "pous," meaning "foot," often appears in scientific and common names as the suffix "-pus," including in the names "octopus" (eight-footed), "platypus" (flat-footed), and "apus" (without foot).

Hemicardium hemicardium — **half-heart cockle.** This saltwater clam of southeastern Asia and Australia gets its scientific name from the Greek words "hemisus," meaning "half," and "kardia," meaning "heart." The name refers to the shape of the clam, which looks like a heart that has been cut in half from the umbo toward the mantle. This species no longer has a tautonymous name and is currently classified as *Lunulicardia hemicardium*.

Irus irus — **irus venus clam.** This Old World saltwater clam is within the family of Venus clams, named after the Roman goddess of love and sexuality. The name "Venus clam" is likely due to artistic portrayals of Venus emerging from a similar shaped scallop shell. The name of this particular species appears to refer to a Greek mythological figure of the same name, either the beggar from The Odyssey or the father of Eurytion in the Peleus story.

Isognomon isognomon — **elongated toothed oyster.** This bivalve mollusk is related to pearl oysters and is found in the Indo-Pacific. Other common names for it include the Pacific toothed oyster and the wader tree oyster. The origin of its scientific name is unclear, but it appears to come from the Greek words "isos," meaning "equal, similar," and "gnomon" or "gnoma" meaning either "know" or "mark." It is unclear why this name would be given. One possibility is that "equal mark" refers to the oyster's hinge teeth, which are equal in size to the width of the shell. This species no longer has a tautonymous name and never really had one—the invalid tautonymous name resulted from a misspelling of the current, near-tautonymous name *Isognomon isognomum.*

Issina issina — **[no common name].** This small saltwater claim is found near the Horn of Africa. The origin of its scientific name is unclear, but it might refer to the Issa people, a northern Somali clan near to Djibouti where the type specimen was collected. Alternatively, it might refer to the *Erycina* genus of mollusks, which was believed to be closely related to this species when this species was named. This species no longer has a tautonymous name and is currently classified as *Thecodonta issina.*

Janthina janthina — **violet sea-snail.** This is a marine gastropod mollusk in the family of purple storm snails. It is found worldwide in the warm waters of tropical and temperate seas, floating at the surface. The scientific name comes from the Latin word, "ianthina," meaning "violet." It maintains its position at the surface by trapping air bubbles in a "bubble raft" made of chitin, a mucous-like substance derivative of glucose.

Koilofera koilofera — **[no common name].** This minute sea snail gets its scientific name from Greek words meaning "bearing a concavity," in reference to the shape of its protoconch whorls.

Kyrina kyrina — **[no common name].** This venerid mollusk can be found in the Gulf of Aden. The origin of the scientific name is unclear and there is little information upon which to make a reliable guess. The name could refer to any of several different, similar words. For example, it might refer to the Greek mythological princess Cyrene, or to the city of northern Africa named after her.

Lambis lambis — **spider conch.** This large sea snail has a flared outer lip that is ornamented with six long, hollow digitations. The origin of its scientific name is unclear, but the word appears to come from the Latin word meaning "to lick, lap, or suck" perhaps in reference to the large lips on this mollusk.

Lataxiena lataxiena — **fimbriate false latiaxis.** This sea snail is a member of the rock snail group and is found in Indonesia. The origin of its scientific name is unclear, but it appears to refer to similarities between species in this genus and those in the genus *Latiaxis*. This species no longer has a tautonymous name and is currently classified as *Lataxiena fimbriata*.

Lima lima — **spiny file clam.** This bivalve mollusk can be found in the Mediterranean Sea, in the eastern Atlantic Ocean, and in Caribbean waters ranging from southern Florida to the West Indies and Bermuda. Its scientific name is the Latin word for "file" (the carpenter's tool). The name appears to be in reference to the many small scales—like teeth on a file—that are on the outside of the shell.

Lionelita lionelita — **[no common name].** This species of small saltwater clam is found in the waters near Djibouti. Its scientific name refers to the name of Lionel Faurot, the person who collected this and many other mollusk specimens for study, including *Faurotis faurotis*. This species no longer has a tautonymous name and is currently classified as *Lionelita nuculoides*.

Lithophaga lithophaga — **date mussel.** This mussel bores into stone or coral rock with the help of pallial gland secretions, hence the scientific name, which comes from the Greek words for "stone" and "eating."

Lutraria lutraria — **otter shell.** The scientific name of this large marine mollusk comes from the Latin name for the otter, "lutra," presumably because otters feed on these animals. For more on the otter's scientific name, see *Lutra lutra.*

Makimonos makimonos — **[no common name].** This sea snail is found off southeastern Africa and off Japan. Its scientific name comes from the Japanese word "makimono," meaning "rolled thing," in reference to the long, spiraling shape of its shell and the fact that the first specimens described were collected from Japan. This species no longer has a tautonymous name and is currently classified as *Tomopleura nivea.*

Malleus malleus — **black hammer oyster.** This hammer-shaped oyster of the Indo-Pacific gets its scientific name from the Latin word "malleus," meaning "hammer."

Margaritifera margaritifera — **freshwater pearl mussel.** This endangered species of freshwater mussel gets its name from the Latin words "margarita," meaning "pearl," and "ferre," meaning "to bear." The interior of its shell has a thick layer of mother of pearl, which allows it to make high-quality pearls. It was recently discovered that the freshwater pearl mussel has negligible senescence, meaning it does not show evidence of biological aging. Scientists have determined that this mussel has a maximum lifespan of 210-250 years.

Martinella martinella — **[no common name].** This carnivorous air-breathing land snail is found in Ecuador. Its scientific name honors the person who collected the specimen that was first described, a Ch. Martin.

Melo melo — **melon shell.** This extremely large sea snail has a huge ovate shell that resembles a melon. It is found in southeastern Asia and is also known as the Indian volute and the bailer shell. The scientific name is the Latin word for a type of melon, likely originating from the Greek word "melopepon" for "melon." This volute is known to produce pearls and is also known to be carnivorous.

Melongena melongena — **Caribbean crown conch.** The scientific name for this large sea snail is the Latin word for "aubergine" (also known as an egg-plant). It is unclear, however, why these snails are named after aubergines. The shells of species within the *Melongena* genus are variable in shape and color. Perhaps one of the earliest crown conches to be named resembled an aubergine in some way. The term "crown conch" is a reference to the crown-like shape of the shell.

Mercenaria mercenaria — **quahog.** This edible marine clam is also known as the hard clam, the round clam, the northern quahog, the chowder clam, and the hard-shelled clam. It is native to the eastern shores of North and Central America. The common name "quahog" comes from the word "poqu-auhock" of the Narragansett language, which is an Algonquian language formerly spoken by the Narragansett people in what is now Rhode Island. Native peoples on the eastern Atlantic seaboard made valuable beads called "wampum" from quahog shells, which were used as money or jewelry. The scientific name comes from the Latin word "mercenarius," from "merces" for "wages," in reference to this shell being used as currency.

Meretrix meretrix — **Asiatic hard clam.** The scientific name of this edible saltwater clam appears to come from the Latin "mereo" and "-trix," meaning "the earner," referring to a prostitute, which is what the word "meretrix" means in English today. It is unclear why this clam would be associated with earners or prostitutes.

Mitella mitella — **Japanese goose barnacle.** This stalked barnacle is found on rocky shores of the Indo-Pacific region. The origin of its scientific name is unclear. The word "mitella" is Latin for "turban" or a bishop's "mitre," but the shape of the barnacle is not obviously similar to those things. Another possibility is that the name is a diminutive form of "mita," Latin for "glove," in reference to mollusk's resemblance to a small hand. Indeed, another common name for this barnacle is "turtle claw." This species no longer has a tautony-mous name and is currently classified as *Capitulum mitella*.

Mitra mitra — **Episcopal miter shell.** This large, predatory sea snail is widespread in the Indo-Pacific from eastern Africa to eastern Polynesia, and from southern Japan to Australia. The scientific and common names for this animal refer to the general shape of the shell, which resembles the miter (in Latin, "mitra"), a type of ceremonial headgear worn by bishops in the Christian tradition.

Modiolus modiolus — **northern horse mussel.** This marine bivalve mollusk is purplish or dark blue in color and robust. The two valves are roughly triangular or bluntly oblong. They are found along the Atlantic and Pacific coasts of North America, and on the European seabed of the Atlantic Ocean from the United Kingdom northwards. The scientific name appears to come from a Latin word meaning either "hub of a wheel" or "small measure of grain," but it is unclear why the mussel would be given this name. In Scottish Gaelic, the species is called "clabaidh-dubha" ("clabby doos"), meaning "big black mouths."

Modulus modulus — **button snail.** This sea snail is found on the coasts of Florida. The name appears to be the Latin word for "a measure," or more specifically, "a small measure," but it is unclear why the snail would have this name. Perhaps the name is a reference to the small size of this animal, which grows up to, but usually smaller than, 16.5 millimeters.

Obesula obesula — **[no common name].** This small sea snail is found in the Pacific Ocean near New Caledonia. Its scientific name comes from the Latin word "obesus," meaning "obese," as the original description of this animal refers to its shell as "solid, oval, and fairly obese."

Ogasawarana ogasawarana — **Ogasawara snail.** This small, tropical snail has an operculum, making it a terrestrial gastropod mollusk. It is named after the Ogasawara Islands south of the Japanese main island chain, and it is endemic to Japan. Its operculum operates like a trapdoor, allowing it to avoid drying out and to protect itself from predators by fully closing the aperture of its shell.

Oliva oliva — **common olive snail.** This sea snail is a member of the olive snail family, Olividae, and gets its scientific name from the Latin word for "olive." Olive snails are known for having smooth, shiny, elongated oval-shaped shells, loosely resembling olives.

Otitoma otitoma — **[no common name].** This sea snail is found in the Red Sea, and off northern Mozambique, Queensland, French Polynesia, the Philippines, and Japan. The origin of its scientific name is unclear and there is little information upon which to make a reliable guess. It could refer to the Ottoman Empire, which once included the region in Djibouti where the type specimen was collected. Of note, the original description named this snail *Otitoma ottitoma*, and subsequent writings about the snail have questioned whether this was a misspelling and whether a tautonym was intended (with either one or two 't's immediately after the first 'o'). This species no longer has a tautonymous name and is currently classified as *Otitoma cyclophora*.

Ovilia ovilia — **[no common name].** The shell of this nutmeg snail was analyzed as a fossil. The origin of its scientific name is unclear and there is little information upon which to make a reliable guess. The name appears to be the Latin word for "sheepfold," meaning an enclosure where sheep are kept. This species no longer has a tautonymous name and is currently classified as *Trigonostoma doliaris*.

Pardalina pardalina — **tortoise dove shell.** This sea snail has a white shell with dark reddish-brown spots. It occurs in the Red Sea, the Indian Ocean off Tanzania, off the Philippines, and in the western Pacific Ocean off Australia. Its scientific name comes from the Latin word "pardalis" meaning "spotted." This species no longer has a tautonymous name and is currently classified as *Pardalinops testudinaria*.

Perna perna — **brown mussel.** This mussel is harvested as a food source and is native to the waters of Africa, Europe, and South America. It grows quickly—making it good for cultivation—and can aggregate in such large amounts that it can sink navigational buoys. The scientific name appears to be the Latin word for "haunch" or "thigh," but it is unclear why this name was given. Perhaps the brown color and overall shape of the mussel is reminiscent of a thighbone with meat on it.

Petalifera petalifera — **petaled petalifera.** This sea slug inhabits the Atlantic Ocean and the Mediterranean Sea. Its scientific name appears to come from the Greek "petalon," meaning "leaf," and the Latin "ferre," meaning "to bear." The name likely refers to the fleshy, wing-like outgrowths or "parapodia" on either side of its body.

Petholatus petholatus — **tapestry turban.** This sea snail has a rich brown shell ornamented in green, yellow, and white markings. It occurs in the Red Sea and the Indian Ocean. The origin of its scientific name is unclear and appears to predate even Carl Linnaeus's description of it. The name appears to refer to the *Macodes petola* plant, the leaves of which bear a beautiful pattern like that which is found on this snail's shell. This species no longer has a tautonymous name and is currently classified as *Turbo petholatus*.

Petitia petitia — **[no common name].** This medium-sized land snail is found in tropical regions of Africa. Its scientific name honors the person who collected the specimen that was used for the original description of this animal, Louis Petit. This species no longer has a tautonymous name and is currently classified as *Leptocala petitia*.

Planorbis planorbis — **common ramshorn snail.** This air-breathing freshwater snail is found in Europe and has a counterclockwise-coiled shell. Its scientific name comes from the Latin words "planus," meaning "flat," and "orbis," meaning "circle," which is descriptive of the shape of its disk-like shell.

Polygyrella polygyrella — **humped coin shell.** This small, air-breathing land snail is found in the northwestern United States. Its scientific name appears to come from the Greek words "poly" and "guros," meaning "many rings," with a diminutive suffix. This might refer to the number of whorls seen on the type specimen or to the ribs or other attributes of the shell. Alternatively, it might be a reference to the larger but similar-looking land snail genus *Polygyra*.

***Pristis pristis* — [no common name].** This bivalve mollusk lives deep in soft sediments in shallow seas. Its scientific name appears to be the Greek word for "saw," in reference to its shell, which was described as being "serrulate" (having small, fine teeth) on both sides. Notably, this tautonym is the same scientific name as that of the common sawfish, *Pristis pristis*. A single name cannot be used to describe multiple animals, so for this and other reasons, this tautonym—which is therefore a "homonym"—is no longer valid. This species is currently classified as *Serratina pristis*.

***Psammosphaerita psammosphaerita* — [no common name].** This medium-sized saltwater clam is found in the Gulf of Aden. Its scientific name comes from the Greek words "psammos," meaning "sand," and "sphaira," meaning "ball." This and other clams in the Psammobiidae family are known as sunset clams due to the vivid pink colors of their shells. This species no longer has a tautonymous name and is currently classified as the near-tautonym *Psammosphaerica psammosphaerita*.

***Pseudamussium pseudamussium* — [no common name].** Whether this name was ever assigned to a species is unclear. There appear to be no scientific sources that recognize *Pseudamussium pseudamussium* as a current or former animal name. Assuming this animal exists within *Pseudamussium*, it is a scallop, and possibly *Pseudamussium peslutrae*. The origin of the scientific name is unclear, and it appears to come from the Greek words "pseudos," meaning "false," and "amussis," meaning "carpenter's ruler." It is not clear why this name would be given to this species.

***Quadrula quadrula* — maple leaf freshwater mussel.** This freshwater mussel native to North America gets its name from the Latin word "quadra," meaning "square," and the diminutive suffix "-ula." The shape of this mussel vaguely resembles a small square. Its common name "maple leaf" presumably comes from the fact that populations of this mussel exist in Manitoba and Ontario in Canada.

Rapa rapa — **bubble turnip.** This sea snail is found near the Indian Ocean off the coasts of Madagascar, the Chagos Archipelago, and Tanzania, and off the coasts of China and the Philippines. Its scientific name is the Latin word for "turnip," presumably in reference to the shape of its shell.

Reneus reneus — **[no common name].** This freshwater mussel is found in western Africa. Its scientific name honors Jules Rene Bourguignat, a malacologist who had just published work on African mollusks when this tautonymous name was assigned. Unfortunately for Mr. Bourguignat and the malacologist who assigned the name, Felix-Pierre Jousseaume, the species had already been discovered and given a different name long before the tautonymous name was given. This species no longer has a tautonymous name and is currently classified as *Coelatura aegyptiaca.*

Retusum retusum — **[no common name].** This predatory sea snail is found in the Indian Ocean. The origin of its scientific name is unclear, but it appears to come from the Latin word "retusus," meaning "blunt," perhaps in reference to the blunt shape of one end of its shell. This species no longer has a tautonymous name and is currently classified as *Ranularia oboesa.*

Sansonia sansonia — **[no common name].** This small sea snail has been found in the waters near Jeddah in Saudi Arabia. Its scientific name refers to the name of the person who collected the type specimen for study, the son of a Professor Sanson. This species no longer has a tautonymous name and is currently classified as *Sansonia andamanica.*

Sarmaticus sarmaticus — **South African turban snail.** This sea snail is abundant off the coast of South Africa. Its scientific name appears to refer to the ancient Sarmatian people of greater Scythia, or to Roman emperor titles boasting conquest of those people, although it is not clear why this name would be given to this snail. This species no longer has a tautonymous name and is currently classified as *Turbo sarmaticus*.

***Savignyarca savignyarca* — oblique ark shell.** This bivalve is found from southern Asia to Japan. The origin of its scientific name is unclear, but it appears to refer to zoologist Marie Jules Cesar Lelorgne de Savigny, with the Latin word "arca" for "ark," in reference to the interior of the shell resembling a wooden boat. This species no longer has a tautonymous name and is currently classified as *Barbatia obliquata*.

***Scintillula scintillula* — [no common name].** This venerid mollusk is found in the waters around Obock in Djibouti. Its scientific name is a Latin word meaning "little spark," although it is not clear why this name would be given. This species no longer has a tautonymous name and is currently classified as *Scintillula lutea*.

***Serrata serrata* — [no common name].** This small sea snail is a member of the margin shell family. The origin of the scientific name is unclear, but it appears to come from the Latin word "serratus," meaning "serrated," perhaps in reference to the lip of its shell, which has small, tooth-like projections.

***Spirula spirula* — ram's horn squid.** This species of deep-water squid-like cephalopod is rarely seen and little is known about it. Its scientific name comes from the Latin word "spira," meaning "coiled," and refers to a spirally coiled, internal, chambered shell that resembles a ram's horn. This shell is the animal's buoyancy organ. Filling different chambers with gas allows it to float and change direction. This deep-water mollusk is also able to emit green light from between the two small fins on its mantle. Its common names also include the little post horn squid and the tail-light squid.

***Staphylaea staphylaea* — stippled cowry.** This sea snail has an oval shell covered in many small, round protuberances. The scientific name comes from the Greek word "staphylo," referring to shapes that resemble clusters like a bunch of grapes, as seen on this snail's shell.

Steeriana steeriana — **malleated door snail.** This land snail is found in Peru. Its scientific name honors zoologist Joseph Beal Steere, who collected the specimen that was first described. This species no longer has a tautonymous name and is currently classified as *Steeriana malleolata*.

Stenotrema stenotrema — **inland slitmout snail.** This air-breathing land snail can be found in the Midwest and southeastern United States. Its shell is covered in short hairs and its opening is a narrow slit. Its scientific name comes from the Greek words "stenos," meaning "narrow," and "trema," meaning "hole," in reference to the small aperture in its shell.

Stolida stolida — **stolid cowrie.** This sea snail is uncommon and has an unusual color pattern on its shell. The base color is blue-grey or tan, with large, irregular brown blotches on the dorsal side. It can be found in the Indian Ocean and the western and central Pacific Ocean along various island coasts. It hides under rocks during the day and emerges at night to feed on sponges and algae. The origin of its scientific name is unclear. The word appears to come from the Latin "stolidus," meaning "stupid, dull," though it is not clear why such a name would be given. Some sources indicate that by the 1800s, shortly after this animal got its name, the word "stolid" came to mean "unemotional, stoic." Again, the reason for this name is not apparent. This species no longer has a tautonymous name and is currently classified as *Bistolida stolida*.

Sunettina sunettina — **[no common name].** This Venus clam is widely distributed in the tropical Indo-West Pacific from the northeastern coast of Africa to southern China and northwestern Australia. Its scientific name appears to come from a pre-Linnaean name for a different mollusk, "le Sunet," which seems to be Old French for "it sounds" or "it blows." This name later became the name of the *Sunetta* genus, which later inspired this clam's scientific name due to similarities observed between it and the *Sunetta* clams. Later, this clam was placed in the *Sunetta* genus and is currently classified as *Sunetta sunettina*.

Tatutor tatutor — [**no common name**]. This tropical land snail was found in what was then known as New Granada, an area in northern South America that now includes Colombia, Ecuador, and Venezuela. The origin of the scientific name is unclear and there is little information upon which to make a reliable guess. The name could refer to any of several different, similar words, including a local vernacular name for this species. This species no longer has a tautonymous name and is currently classified as *Thaumastus tatutor*.

Telescopium telescopium — **telescope snail.** This cone-shaped sea snail has a distinctive shell that gives it its scientific name, which is Latin for "telescope." The snail has three eyes and can store saved oxygen for up to 48 hours before dying. This snail has also been used by humans for various purposes, including as bio monitors of certain metals in tropical intertidal regions, as a food source in southeastern Asia, and as part of some asthma medications. Some studies have even suggested that when eaten, this snail's tissue can act as a central nervous system depressant.

Terebellum terebellum — **terebellum conch.** This sea snail gets its scientific name from the Latin word for "borer" or "auger" in reference to the long, thin, pointed shape of this animal's shell.

Tergipes tergipes — [**no common name**]. This species of aeolid nudibranch sea slug has brightly colored protruding organs on its back that aid in respiration. The scientific name "tergipes" is difficult to trace, but it may come from the Latin word "tergum," meaning "back" or "rear" in reference to the animal's unusual dorsal surface.

Tesselata tesselata — **checkerboard cowrie.** This sea snail, a cowrie, has a shiny shell with light and dark brown markings in a pattern that loosely resembles a checkerboard. It is found in southeastern Asia and Hawaii. Its scientific name comes from the Latin word "tessellatus," meaning "tessellated" or "checkered," in reference to its shell. Other scientific names assigned to this animal include *Tessellata tessellata* (a tautonym) and *Tesselata tessellata* (a near-tautonym). This species no longer has a tautonymous name and is currently classified as *Luria tessellata*.

Tricornis tricornis — **three-cornered conch.** This sea snail can be found in the Red Sea, the Gulf of Aden, and the Indian Ocean. Its scientific name is the Latin word meaning "three-horned," and refers to the three horns on its shell.

Trigonostoma trigonostoma — **triangular nutmeg.** This sea snail is a member of the nutmeg snail family and is found in Sri Lanka, the Philippines, and Australia. Its scientific name comes from the Greek words "trigonon" and "stoma," and refers to the animal's "triangular mouth." This species no longer has a tautonymous name and is currently classified as *Trigonostoma scalare*.

Tugonella tugonella — **[no common name].** This clam is found in the Philippines. Its scientific name comes from a pre-Linnaean name for a mollusk, "le Tugon," the meaning of which is unclear and appears to come from Old French. It is possible that the name refers to a city in the Philippines or to a Tagalog word, but this seems unlikely given that the name apparently originated in connection with a study of mollusks in Senegal, not the Philippines. This species no longer has a tautonymous name and is currently classified as *Tugonia decurtata*.

Umbraculum umbraculum — **umbrella slug.** This large, strange-looking sea snail is found in tropical and warm parts of the Indo-Pacific and Atlantic oceans where it feeds on sponges. It grows up to 8 inches long. The common name and the scientific name, which come from the Latin word for "umbrella," refer to the relatively small external shell on the snail's dorsal surface. The shell is a flattish cone resembling a small umbrella over the snail.

Varicopeza varicopeza — **[no common name].** This sea snail is found in the waters of the Philippines and Australia. Its scientific name appears to come from the Latin words "varicare," meaning "to straddle," and "pes," meaning "foot," possibly in reference to the shape or movement of this snail's foot.

This species no longer has a tautonymous name and is currently classified as *Varicopeza pauxilla*.

***Velutina velutina* — velvet shell.** This small sea snail has a thin, transparent shell with a velvety epidermis and gets its scientific name from the Latin word "velutinus" for "velvety."

***Ventrilia ventrilia* — [no common name].** This nutmeg snail appears to have existed during the Pliocene epoch. The origin of its scientific name is unclear and there is little information upon which to make a reliable guess. It could come from the Latin word "venter," for "stomach," but the reason for this name is not clear. This species no longer has a tautonymous name and is currently classified as *Ventrilia tenerum*.

***Verticordia verticordia* — [no common name].** Whether this name was ever assigned to a species is unclear. There appear to be no scientific sources that recognize *Verticordia verticordia* as a current or former animal name. Assuming this animal exists within *Verticordia*, it is a clam in the family Verticordiidae. The name appears to come from the Latin word meaning "changer of hearts," an epithet of the Roman goddess Venus. The association between the goddess Venus and clam or scallop shells is seen in the family name Veneridae, which includes the tautonymous species *Irus irus*.

***Villosa villosa* — [no common name].** The scientific name of this fresh-water mussel found in southeastern North America is difficult to trace. The word "villosa" is Latin for "hairy," but this mollusk is not hairy. Perhaps the ray-like pattern on the shell of the mussels was reminiscent of hair to those who first described them, or perhaps the moss that grows on its shell has a "shaggy" appearance. Notably, many of the mussels in the *Villosa* genus have been reclassified in recent years, and the genus went from having 15 species to only four.

Viviparus viviparus — **European freshwater snail.** This large freshwater snail is found in Europe, as indicated by the common name. Its scientific name, from Latin, refers to the unusual method among snails for giving birth to live young after producing eggs that hatch internally.

Volva volva — **shuttlecock volva.** This sea snail is found in the Pacific and Indian oceans. The shape of its shell is unusual with the body whorl being only one third the length of the shell and the canals on each end being fairly long. The origin of its scientific name is unclear, but it likely comes from the Latin word for "wrapper" or "cover" in reference to its unusually long shell.

Vulsella vulsella — **sponge finger clam.** This Indo-Pacific clam has evolved a symbiotic relationship with a sponge. The clam hides deeply embedded in the sponge with only a small opening of its shell on the surface of the sponge, and in return for the protection that the sponge provides, the clam pushes water deep into the sponge, allowing the sponge to grow faster. The origin of its scientific name is unclear. It might come from the Latin word "vulsus" for "plucked, shorn," with a diminutive suffix, or it might refer to the word "vulsellum" for a type of forceps. It is not clear why either of these terms would be used to refer to this clam.

Zonaria zonaria — **zoned cowrie.** This small sea snail is found in the Atlantic Ocean. The origin of the scientific name is unclear and there is little information upon which to make a reliable guess. The name appears to come from the Latin word for "a belt or girdle," in which case it may refer to the red and yellow bands or stripes that are seen on its shell.

PART IX:

WORMS, SPONGES, CNIDARIANS, AND OTHERS

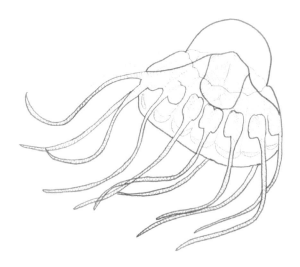

Periphylla periphylla

THE ANIMALS IN THIS CATEGORY include a wide range of worms, sea sponges, jellyfish, hydrozoans, sea urchins, and others. These groups are similar only in that they are dissimilar to the chordates, arthropods, and mollusks listed in the prior sections. As with many arthropods, the etymological origins for some of these species are difficult to determine and should be accepted cautiously. Of note, the species in this list include the longest tautonyms, two of which are 34 letters each. They also include the shortest tautonyms, two of which of which are six letters each.

Aaptos aaptos — **[no common name]**. This toxic sea sponge contains an adrenoreceptor-blocking compound that is highly toxic to fish. Its scientific name is Greek for "invincible" or "unapproachable," apparently in reference to the consistency of the sponge, which is very firm and compact. Alternatively, the name could be in reference to the sponge's toxicity, making it inedible by many would-be predators. Not much is known about this animal.

Abbreviata abbreviata — **[no common name]**. This parasitic nematode finds hosts in various European and African lizard species. The origin of its scientific name is difficult to trace, but it may come from the Latin word "abbreviatus," meaning "shortened," in reference to the anatomy of this nematode, which was originally described as having a short tail and a small gallbladder.

Acanthogyrus acanthogyrus — **[no common name]**. This parasitic worm is found in Africa and southern Asia. It has been found living in the intestines of different carp species in India, including the tautonymous *Catla catla*. The scientific name appears to come from the Greek word "acantha," meaning "thorn," and "guros," meaning "ring." The phylum Acanthocephala, which includes this species, is so named because its "thorny-headed worms" have proboscises armed with spines that they use to pierce and hold the gut walls of their host animals. Thorny-headed worms like this one are thought to engage in control of their hosts by changing serotonin levels in the host brains. For instance, it is believed that thorny-headed worms will occupy small gammarid crustaceans and cause their serotonin levels to rise massively. This increase in serotonin corresponds to gammarids leaving the safety of the pond or river floor, moving to the surface, and waiting to be eaten by ducks. This allows the thorny-headed worm to enter its final host, the duck. This behavior is known as "brain-jacking."

Anchoradiscus anchoradiscus — [**no common name**]. This trematode, also known as a fluke, is parasitic on North American sunfishes. Its scientific name comes from the Latin words "ancora," meaning "anchor," and "discus," meaning "disk," likely in reference to its disk-shaped haptor, which is an organ that allows it to attach—or anchor—itself to its host. This species no longer has a tautonymous name and is currently classified as *Anchoradiscus triangularis*.

Archigyrodactylus archigyrodactylus — [**no common name**]. This parasitic tapeworm finds hosts in gibbons. The origin of its scientific name is difficult to trace but appears to relate to the similarity between this species and those in the genus *Gyrodactylus*. Translated literally from Greek, the name means something like "chief" or "governing," "ring," and "finger," perhaps in reference to the shape of its body or its anchor organs. This scientific name is tied for the longest tautonym.

Brissus brissus — **groove burrowing sea urchin.** This sea urchin is grey in color and has an armor that is covered in small spines, giving it a furry appearance. The scientific name appears to come from the word "bryssus," used by Aristotle in his *Historia Animalium*, where he describes several species of urchins. According to the naturalist that first described this species, the word "bryssus" is a corrupted version of another Greek word that means "not suitable for eating." This species no longer has a tautonymous name and is currently classified as *Brissus unicolor*.

Cephea cephea — **crowned jellyfish.** This jellyfish lives in the tropical waters of the western Indo-Pacific to northern Australia. Although this species is among the most venomous jellyfish, it is not harmful to humans and is eaten as a delicacy and used for medical purposes in China and Japan. It is purplish-blue in color, grows up to 60 centimeters in diameter, and uses its tentacles to stun, kill, and grapple its prey items. The origin of its scientific name is unclear, but it is probably in reference to the Greek mythological king, Cepheus, who features prominently in the legend of Perseus. According to the myth, Cepheus's wife angered Poseidon, who sent a flood and a sea monster to destroy Cepheus's city. The only way to stop the destruction was for Cepheus to offer up his daughter, Andromeda, to the monster. Andromeda was saved from this fate by Perseus, who used the severed head of Medusa to turn the monster to stone. It is not clear why the Cepheidae jellyfish would be named after King Cepheus. Perhaps it is because they appear to have crowns, like a king would wear, hence the common name "crowned jellyfish." When this species was originally described in 1775, it was given the name *Medusa cephea*, evincing a fairly clear link to the myth of Perseus, Cepheus, and Medusa.

***Chaos chaos* — giant amoeba.** Strangely, this organism's name itself has a chaotic history, making the name autological as well. Over the course of roughly 265 years, biologists have used different names at different times and places to describe this organism, causing mass confusion as to what it is called. In 1755, the amoeboid was first described as "the little Proteus." Three years later, Carl Linnaeus gave it the scientific name *Volvox chaos*. However, because the name *Volvox* had already been applied to a genus of algae, he later changed it to *Chaos chaos*. In 1879, all the large, freshwater amoebae were reclassified into one species called *Amoeba proteus*. A dozen species names, including several within *Chaos*, were to be regarded as synonyms of *Amoeba proteus*. However, in 1900 it was discovered that one organism within *Amoeba proteus* had hundreds of cellular nuclei. Since there already existed a genus of giant multinucleate amoebae, *Pelomyxa*, the organism was reclassified from *Amoeba proteus* to *Pelomyxa carolinensis*. In 1926, it was discovered that *Pelomyxa carolinensis* was, in fact, identical to the amoeba that had been described in 1755 as "the little Proteus," which Linnaeus had named *Chaos chaos*. Therefore, the name was changed back to *Chaos chaos*. This became the subject of great debate. Many scientists argued against the validity of that name, but others adopted it. A third faction accepted the genus *Chaos* for the amoeba, but retained the specific name *carolinensis*, referring to the organism as *Chaos carolinensis*. By the early 1970s, all three names were in use concurrently, leading to more confusion. However, as more has been discovered about the organism, a consensus has emerged, and today the organism is generally known as *Chaos carolinensis*, as first proposed in 1948. The organism has also been placed in the taxon Amoebozoa, a distinct sister group to the Animalia kingdom. The word "chaos" in Greek means "abyss," and also refers to the abyss of Tartarus, the Greek mythological underworld. The common names of this species are also somewhat chaotic, with one of them indicating that it is large ("giant amoeba") and the other indicating that it is small ("little Proteus").

Charcotus charcotus — **[no common name]**. This echiuroid worm is found in the Atlantic Ocean. Its scientific name refers to the ship "J. Charcot," which surveyed the Atlantic Ocean in December of 1978 and allowed biologists to collect several new annelid species, including this one.

Cidaris cidaris — **long-spine slate pen sea urchin.** This sea urchin is found in deep water in the eastern Atlantic Ocean and the Mediterranean Sea. Its scientific name comes from the Greek word "kidaris," referring to a royal headdress or tiara of ancient Persian kings. The urchin's long and widely spaced spines are reminiscent of the ancient crowns.

Convoluta convoluta — **[no common name]**. This very small acoel flatworm likely gets its scientific name from the Latin word "convolutus" meaning "rolled up together," possibly in reference to the worm's body-wall muscu-lature, which is composed of circular muscle fibers. The order name Acoela comes from a Greek word meaning "absence of cavity" in reference to the fact that this worm does not have a fluid-filled body cavity.

Crambe crambe — **orange-red encrusting sponge.** This bright orange sponge is endemic to the Mediterranean Sea and is also found in the north-ern Atlantic Ocean. Its scientific name appears to come from the Greek word "krambe" for "cabbage," in reference to shape of sponges in the Crambeidae family.

Echiurus echiurus — **[no common name]**. The scientific name of this echi-urid spoon worm comes from the Greek words meaning "viper tail," which refers to the rows of golden spines sticking out of its posterior side. This worm has a large, extendible, scoop-shaped proboscis in front of its mouth, which is why it is known as a spoon worm. A different spoon worm, *Urechis unicinctus*, is known by the common names "fat innkeeper worm" and "Chinese penis fish."

Gracilisentis gracilisentis — **[no common name].** This parasite belongs to the phylum Acanthocephala, or "thorny-headed" worms. Its scientific name appears to come from the Latin words "gracilis" and "ens," meaning "to be slender," perhaps in reference to the shape of its body.

Halecium halecium — **herringbone hydroid.** This hydrozoan is native to the Atlantic Ocean and the eastern Pacific Ocean. The growth pattern of its branches gives it a herringbone-like appearance. Its scientific name comes from the Latin word "halex," for "herring," in reference to the similarity of this animal's shape to the herringbone pattern in a herring fish's spine. This species no longer has a tautonymous name and is currently classified as *Halecium halecinum*. The tautonymous name was apparently the result of a misspelling.

Hamigera hamigera — **[no common name].** This sponge is found in the Mediterranean Sea. Its common name comes from the Latin word "hamus" for "hook," in reference to hook-like shapes that appear on the surface of this sponge.

Heterophyes heterophyes — **Egyptian mummy intestinal fluke.** This parasite was discovered in 1851 during an autopsy of an Egyptian mummy. They are found in the Middle East, Africa, and western Europe. They use different host animals to complete their lifecycle, including snails, fish, and humans and other mammals. The scientific name comes from Greek and roughly translates to "different growth" or "different original form," which is in reference to the fact that this species differs from the flukes in the genus *Paragonimus*. They come into contact with humans who eat contaminated or raw fish.

Hormiphora hormiphora — **[no common name].** This comb jelly is found in the western Atlantic Ocean. The origin of its scientific name is unclear, but it appears to come from the Greek prefix "horm-," meaning "that which excites," and the suffix "-phoros," meaning "bearing," perhaps in reference to the exciting, shimmering rainbow color that its cilia produce when swimming.

Icelanonchohaptor icelanonchohaptor — **[no common name].** This species is a flatworm, which is a simple, unsegmented, soft-bodied invertebrate. Its scientific name comes from the Greek work "ikelos," meaning "resembling," and translates to "resembling *Anonchohaptor*," which is a different flatworm genus. This scientific name is tied for the longest tautonym.

Jia jia — **[no common name].** This sponge is found off the western coast of the United States. Its scientific name appears to come from the simple fact that part of the sponge's anatomy—its smaller spicules—are shaped like the letter "J." The naturalist who first described this sponge explained that the *Jia* genus "may be characterized by peculiar microscleres shaped like the letter J, one end blunt and the other of ultimate fineness." This species no longer has a tautonymous name and is currently classified as *Antho jia*. The scientific name *Jia jia* is tied for the shortest tautonym.

Loa loa — **eye worm.** This animal is a parasitic nematode found in western and central Africa. Its scientific name means "worm" in an African language (likely Angolan). This species is known as the "eye worm" because of the disease it causes, Loa loa filariasis, which can cause pain and swelling in human eyes. The adult *Loa loa* is carried to humans through the bite of a deer fly or mango fly. The disease is among the so-called "neglected diseases," a group of tropical infections that are common in low-income populations of developing regions of Africa, Asia, and the Americas. This scientific name is tied for the shortest tautonym.

Microchaetus microchaetus — **[no common name].** This giant earthworm gets its scientific name from the Greek words "mikros" and "khaite" meaning "small hairs," which refers to the small bristles on the worm's body that help it to move around. The largest species of earthworm is *Microchaetus rappi* of South Africa, which reaches an average length of 6 feet and has been recorded at 21 feet long.

Moniliformis moniliformis — [no common name]. This parasitic worm is usually found in intestines of rodents or carnivores like cats and dogs. As with other parasitic worms, this species engages in "brain-jacking" by inducing a behavioral change in its intermediate host that increases the risk of predation by a later host. This helps the parasite by increasing its chances of getting to its final, "definitive" host. These worms can infest humans, but this is rare as it would require a human to eat a raw, infested beetle or cockroach. The scientific name appears to come from the Latin words "monile" and "formis," meaning "having the form of a necklace." The worm itself is long and appears to have many segments, not unlike a necklace.

Multiceps multiceps — [no common name]. This species of tapeworm lives in the small intestines of canids. Its scientific name comes from the Latin words meaning "many" and "head," in reference to the many suckers and hooks that this species develops in its larval stage. This species no longer has a tautonymous name and is currently classified as *Taenia multiceps*.

Oncicola oncicola — [no common name]. This parasitic worm can be found in terrestrial vertebrates. Its scientific name comes from the Greek word "onkos" and the Latin suffix "-cola" meaning "one who hooks," in reference to the manner in which it attaches itself to the intestinal walls of its host.

Ophiura ophiura — serpent star. This strange-looking creature is similar to a starfish, but it has long, whip-like arms that help it swim and travel across the sea floor with jerky motions. It is found on coastal seabeds in northwestern Europe. It can burrow for protection, and it can regenerate its arms if they are damaged or torn off. This animal's scientific name comes from the Greek words "ophis," for "serpent," and "oura," for "tail," referring to its serpent-like arms.

Periphylla periphylla — **helmet jellyfish.** This deep-sea jellyfish is found in nearly every ocean of the world. It is the only species of the genus *Periphylla*, and it is capable of lighting itself from within by means of bioluminescence. Its scientific name translated from Greek means "around leaves." This may be in reference to the lappets (flaps) that sway back and forth along the bottom edge of its bell.

Pilum pilum — **[no common name].** This parasitic worm attaches itself to freshwater fishes of the southeastern United States. Its scientific name comes from the Latin word for "javelin" and refers to the long, pear-like shape of the worm's proboscis.

Porites porites — **hump coral.** This species of stony coral is found in the Caribbean Sea and the Atlantic Ocean. It is also known as finger coral because it forms short, finger-like lobes. Individuals of this species are thought to be some of the oldest lifeforms on earth due to their slow growth rate. The scientific name appears to come from the Latin word "porus" for "pore," in reference to the body of the coral being porous.

Porpita porpita — **blue button.** This marine organism consists of a circular float organ and a colony of hydroids, which are small creatures similar to jellyfish. They are found in warmer, tropical and sub-tropical waters. The hard, brown float is almost flat and is about 1 inch wide. The float organ is responsible for the organism's vertical movement and contains pores that can communicate with other *Porpita porpita* organisms. The hydroid colony, which can range from bright blue turquoise to yellow, resembles tentacles like those of a jellyfish and can sting. The blue button sting is not powerful but may cause slight irritation to human skin. In recent years, it has been hypothesized that due to global warming, the species has begun appearing in larger numbers along coastlines in Japan. The scientific name comes from the Greek word for brooch, a decorative piece of jewelry used to fasten garments together.

Pyragraphorus pyragraphorus — **[no common name].** This flatworm appears to get its scientific name from the Greek words "pur," meaning "fire," and "graphia," meaning "writing." Pyrography is a method of decorating wood, leather, or other materials with burn marks. The reason for the scientific name is not clear, but it may refer to the worm's clamp appendages, which are shaped like "fire-tongs."

Quinqueserialis quinqueserialis — **[no common name].** This trematode infects muskrats in North America and appears to get its scientific name from the Latin words "quinque" and "series," meaning "five rows," possibly in reference to its five rows of ventral papillae.

Rhabdosynochus rhabdosynochus — **[no common name].** This flatworm gets its scientific name from the Greek words "rhabdos," meaning "rod," and "sunokhos," meaning "joined together," possibly in reference to its long, rod-shaped body.

Rhamnocercus rhamnocercus — **[no common name].** This flatworm is a parasite of croaker fishes. Its scientific name appears to come from the Greek words "rhamnos," meaning "buckthorn," and "kerkos," meaning "tail," possibly in reference to the shape of its tail.

Sergia sergia — **[no common name].** This flatworm gets its scientific name from the monastery Sergijewa Pustyn, which is near to the Gulf of Finland where the species was discovered.

Spirorbis spirorbis — **coiled bristle worm.** These little annelid worms live attached to seaweed and eel grass in shallow saltwater. Their orange bodies are encased in white, left-handed coiled shells. The scientific name comes from the Latin words "spira," meaning "coiled," and "orbis," meaning "disk."

Syringella syringella — **[no common name].** This species of sponge is found in the Mediterranean Sea. Its scientific name appears to come from the Greek word "surinx," meaning "tube, pipe," possibly in reference to the sponge's system of canals and chambers through which water passes. This species no longer has a tautonymous name and is currently classified as *Suberites syringella*.

***Thalassema thalassema* — Gaertner's spoon worm.** This unsegmented, soft-bodied spoon worm grows up to 7 centimeters in length and its trunk may be blue, grey, yellow, pink, or purple in color. Its scientific name appears to come from the Greek word "thalassa," for "sea," in reference to the fact that this spoon worm was discovered living among crevices of sea cliffs in Cornwall.

***Tubifex tubifex* — sludge worm.** This creature is a segmented worm that inhabits the sediments of lakes and rivers on several continents and can occasionally be found in sewer lines. The scientific name comes from the Latin words "tubus" for "tube," and "facere" for "to make." In 2009, a large mass of *Tubifex* colonies was discovered in the sewers of Raleigh, North Carolina. Videos of the creature went viral on the internet under the name "Carolina poop monster."

***Turgida turgida* — [no common name].** This nematode is a common parasite of the stomachs of Virginia opossums. It reaches opossums through intermediate hosts, such as cockroaches. The origin of its scientific name is unclear, but it appears to come from the Latin word "turgidus," meaning "swollen" or "distended," possibly in reference to this nematode's sponge-like body, or to the effects it has on opossum stomachs.

***Velella velella* — by-the-wind sailor.** This creature is a free-floating hydrozoan that lives on the surface of the open ocean. It can be found in warm and temperate waters in all the world's oceans. It is also known as the sea raft, the purple sail, and the little sail. Its common and scientific names refer to the little stiff sail on its top that catches the wind and propels it over the surface of the water. The word "velella" comes from the Latin word "velum," meaning "sail."

PART X:

BIBLIOGRAPHY AND APPENDIX

BIBLIOGRAPHY

FOR NEARLY EVERY ENTRY INCLUDED in this book, the original scientific description of the animal and its subsequent reclassification documents, if any, were reviewed in determining how to describe the animal and its name. Those thousands of works are not listed below but are publicly available and easily found through sources like the Biodiversity Heritage Library. Many online and print sources were consulted for supporting facts and fact-checking, including Wikipedia, Wiktionary, Wikispecies, the Encyclopedia of Life, the Integrated Taxonomic Information System, the Merriam-Webster Online Dictionary, and the Online Etymology Dictionary. Information found in these sources was verified using the source material from their articles and other, independent sources. In addition, the following principal sources were used, and the author of this book is indebted to the thoughtful research conducted by the teams and individuals that created or contributed to them.

A.F. Gotch, Latin Names Explained: A Guide to the Scientific Classification of Reptiles, Birds & Mammals (1995).

Andy Warren, et al., Butterflies of America, https://www.butterfliesofamerica.com/index.html.

Biodiversity Heritage Library, https://www.biodiversitylibrary.org/.

Buchanan, R. E., et al., Proposed Bacteriological Code of Nomenclature, Developed from proposals approved by International Committee on Bacteriological Nomenclature at the Meeting of the Third International Congress for Microbiology (1947).

Buchanan R. E., et al., International Bacteriological Code of Nomenclature, Journal of Bacteriology, Vol. 55 (1948).

Butterflies of the World, https://www.learnaboutbutterflies.com.

C.M. Cooper et al., Successful Proof of Concept of Family Planning and Immunization Integration in Liberia, Global Health: Science and Practice, Vol. 3 (2015).

Carl Linnaeus, Systema Naturae, First Edition (1735).

Carl Linnaeus, Systema Naturae, Tenth Edition (1758).

Charles Darwin, On the Origin of Species by Means of Natural Selection, or Preservation of Favoured Races in the Struggle for Life (1859).

Christopher Scharpf, The ETYFish Project, https://etyfish.org/.

Darryl Francis, A Ten-Letter Tautonym List, Word Ways, Vol. 15, Iss. 4 (1982).

Edward R. Wolpow, Triple Tautonyms in Biology, Word Ways, Vol. 16, Iss. 2 (1983).

Encyclopedia of Life, https://eol.org/.

Fishbase, https://www.fishbase.se/search.php.

Georgina M. Mace, The Role of Taxonomy in Species Conservation, Philos. Trans. R. Soc. Lond. B. Biol. Sci. (2004).

Global Biodiversity Information Facility, https://www.gbif.org/.

Guha Krishnamurthi, Making a Legal Academic, Texas Law Review Online, Vol. 100 (2021-2022) ("Precision is no man's enemy.").

H.E. Strickland, et al., Report of a Committee appointed "to consider of the rules by which the Nomenclature of Zoology may be established on a Uniform and Permanent Basis," Report of 12th Meeting of the British Association for the Advancement of Science, June 1842 (1843).

H.E. Strickland, Rules for Zoological Nomenclature (1878)

Harold N. Moldenke, A Discussion of Tautonyms, Bulletin of the Torrey Botanical Club, Vol. 59, No. 3 (1932).

Integrated Taxonomic Information System, https://itis.gov/.

International Botanical Conference of Vienna 1905, International rules of Botanical Nomenclature (1906).

International Botanical Congress, Laws of botanical nomenclature, ed. 2 (1883).

International Botanical Congress, International rules of botanical nomenclature (1935).

International Commission for the Nomenclature of Cultivated Plants, International Code of Nomenclature for Cultivated Plants (2009).

International Commission on Zoological Nomenclature, International Code of Zoological Nomenclature: adopted by the XV International Congress of Zoology (1961).

International Commission on Zoological Nomenclature, International Code of Zoological Nomenclature, Second Edition (1964).

International Commission on Zoological Nomenclature, International Code of Zoological Nomenclature, Third Edition (1985).

International Commission on Zoological Nomenclature, International Code of Zoological Nomenclature, Fourth Edition (1999).

International Committee on Bacteriological Nomenclature, International Code of Nomenclature of Bacteria and Viruses (1958).

International Committee on Taxonomy of Viruses, International Code of Virus Classification and Nomenclature (2021).

James A. Jobling, The Helm Dictionary of Scientific Bird Names (2010).

Jon Reidy, The Problem of 'Proceeds' in the Era of FERA, American Journal of Criminal Law, Vol. 37 (2010) ("Precision is no man's enemy . . . .").

Kevin De Queiroz, Species Concepts and Species Delimitation, Systematic Biology, Vol. 56, Iss. 6, (2007).

Lapage, S.P., et al., International Code of Nomenclature of Bacteria (1975).

Lapage, S.P., et al., International Code of Nomenclature of Bacteria (1992).

Leo J. Van Gemert & Abraham S.H. Breure, The Tautonyms of Jousseaume: A Taxonomical Study, Folia Conchyliologica, No. 42 (2017).

Mark Isaak, Curiosities of Biological Nomenclature, https://www.curioustaxonomy.net/index.html.

Markku Savela, Lepidoptera and Some Other Life Forms, https://www.nic.funet.fi/pub/sci/bio/life/intro.html.

Michael J. Stephan, (203–205) Proposals to require initial lowercase letters for specific and infraspecific epithets, to permit tautonyms non-retroactively, and to use consistent language in Articles 20.1 and 23.2, TAXON, Vol. 72: 446-447 (2023) (https://doi.org/10.1002/tax.12902).

Megan Shersby, Guide to Tautonyms, Triple Tautonyms, and Binomial Nomenclature, BBC Wildlife Magazine (2021).

Merriam-Webster Online Dictionary, https://www.merriam-webster.com/.

N. J. Turland, et al., International Code of Nomenclature for algae, fungi, and plants (Shenzhen Code) adopted by the Nineteenth International Botanical Congress July 2017 (2018).

Natural History Museum, Butterflies and Moths of the World: Generic Names and Their Type-Species, https://www.nhm.ac.uk/our-science/data/butmoth/.

Online Etymology Dictionary, https://www.etymonline.com/.

Parker, C.T., et al., International Code of Nomenclature of Prokaryotes (2008 Revision), International Journal of Systematic and Evolutionary Microbiology, Vol. 69 (2019).

R. Blanchard, et al., International Rules of Zoological Nomenclature (1905).

Roland Wilbur Brown, Composition of Scientific Words (1956).

Samuel S. Long, Tautonyms in Biology (Parts 1-2), Word Ways, Vol. 29, Iss. 3-4 (1996).

Tim Williams, A Dictionary of the Roots and Combining Forms of Scientific Words (2005).

W.H. Evans, A Catalogue of the American Hesperiidae (1951-1955).

Wikiaves, https://www.wikiaves.com.br/.

Wikipedia, https://en.wikipedia.org/.

Wikispecies, https://species.wikimedia.org/.

Wiktionary, https://www.wiktionary.org/.

World Register of Marine Species, https://www.marinespecies.org/index.php.

APPENDIX

Cardinalis cardinalis

LIST OF MAMMAL TAUTONYMOUS TRINOMIALS

As with the lists of tautonyms, this list includes names that are no longer considered valid, or may never have been considered valid, but that appeared in at least one reliable source. The common name of the species is in parentheses. If the subspecies also has a common name, it is indicated after the common name of the species. A single asterisk (*) indicates that the tautonymous trinomial is not currently considered valid either because the species has been renamed and no longer has a tautonymous name, or because it never had a valid tautonymous name in the first instance. A double asterisk (**) indicates that the validity of the subspecies division is subject to debate. Both types of issues are addressed in the longer descriptions of the tautonyms set forth above.

1. *Alces alces alces* (moose, European elk)

2. *Axis axis axis* (chital deer, Indian chital deer)

3. *Barbastella barbastella barbastella* (western barbastelle bat)*

4. *Bison bison bison* (American bison, Plains bison)

5. *Capreolus capreolus capreolus* (roe deer, common European roe deer)

6. *Caracal caracal caracal* (caracal, southern caracal)

7. *Chinchilla chinchilla chinchilla* (short-tailed chinchilla)

8. *Citellus citellus citellus* (European ground squirrel)*

9. *Cricetus cricetus cricetus* (common hamster)

10. *Crocuta crocuta crocuta* (spotted hyena)

11. *Dama dama dama* (fallow deer, European fallow deer)

12. *Gazella gazella gazella* (mountain gazelle)

13. *Genetta genetta genetta* (common genet)

14. *Gerbillus gerbillus gerbillus* (lesser Egyptian gerbil)

15. *Giraffa giraffa giraffa* (southern giraffe)

16. *Glis glis glis* (edible dormouse)

17. *Gorilla gorilla gorilla* (western gorilla, western lowland gorilla)

18. *Gulo gulo gulo* (wolverine, Old World wolverine)

19. *Hoolock hoolock hoolock* (western hoolock gibbon)

20. *Hyaena hyaena hyaena* (striped hyena, Indian striped hyena)**

21. *Indri indri indri* (indri)**

22. *Jaculus jaculus jaculus* (lesser Egyptian jerboa)

23. ***Lagurus lagurus lagurus*** (steppe vole)

24. ***Lemmus lemmus lemmus*** (Norwegian lemming, common Norwegian lemming)

25. ***Leo leo leo*** (African lion)*

26. ***Lutra lutra lutra*** (Eurasian otter)

27. ***Lynx lynx lynx*** (Eurasian lynx, northern lynx)

28. ***Marmota marmota marmota*** (alpine marmot)

29. ***Martes martes martes*** (pine marten)

30. ***Megantereon megantereon megantereon*** (no common name)*

31. ***Meles meles meles*** (European badger)

32. ***Mephitis mephitis mephitis*** (striped skunk, Canada striped skunk)

33. ***Molossus molossus molossus*** (velvety free-tailed bat)

34. ***Myospalax myospalax myospalax*** (Siberian zokor)

35. ***Myotis myotis myotis*** (greater mouse-eared bat)

36. ***Nasua nasua nasua*** (South American coati)

37. ***Niviventer niviventer niviventer*** (white-bellied rat)

38. ***Oreotragus oreotragus oreotragus*** (klipspringer, Cape klipspringer)

39. ***Panthera panthera panthera*** (leopard, Barbary leopard)*

40. ***Petaurista petaurista petaurista*** (red giant flying squirrel)

41. ***Phocoena phocoena phocoena*** (harbor porpoise)

42. ***Pipistrellus pipistrellus pipistrellus*** (common pipistrelle)**

43. ***Pithecia pithecia pithecia*** (white-faced saki)**

44. ***Putorius putorius putorius*** (European polecat)*

45. ***Rattus rattus rattus*** (black rat, roof rat)**

46. ***Redunca redunca redunca*** (bohor reedbuck)

47. ***Rupicapra rupicapra rupicapra*** (chamois, Apline chamois)

48. ***Saccolaimus saccolaimus saccolaimus*** (naked-rumped pouched bat)

49. ***Strepsiceros strepsiceros strepsiceros*** (greater kudu)*

50. ***Uncia uncia uncia*** (snow leopard)*

51. ***Vicugna vicugna vicugna*** (vicuna)*

52. ***Vulpes vulpes vulpes*** (red fox, Scandinavian red fox)

MAJOR TAXONOMIC RANKS

The hierarchy of the major taxonomic ranks in biological classification is as follows, with some examples. Intermediate minor ranks are not shown.

	red fox	common pipistrelle	Eurasian eagle-owl	Ogasawara snail
Domain	Eukaryota	Eukaryota	Eukaryota	Eukaryota
Kingdom	Animalia	Animalia	Animalia	Animalia
Phylum	Chordata	Chordata	Chordata	Mollusca
Class	Mammalia	Mammalia	Aves	Gastropoda
Order	Carnivora	Chiroptera	Strigiformes	Cycloneritida
Family	Canidae	Vespertilionidae	Strigidae	Helicinidae
Genus	*Vulpes*	*Pipistrellus*	*Bubo*	*Ogasawarana*
Species	*vulpes*	*pipistrellus*	*bubo*	*ogasawarana*

TAUTONYMOUS NAMES CREATED FROM BINOMIAL FORMATION OF TERMS IN *SYSTEMA NATURAE*, FIRST EDITION (1735)

Carl Linnaeus's first edition of *Systema Naturae* is an eleven-page document, two pages of which are devoted to animal names. The catalogue of animals is organized in tables with several columns and rows, including columns for "Genera" and "Species." The following names can be formed by combining terms from those two columns into binomial-style scientific names.

Use of binomial nomenclature did not become standardized until 1758, which was 23 years after this edition of *Systema Naturae* was published. By that time, many of the names of these animals had changed. For instance, the *Canis* genus was significantly revised, and *Canis Canis* (dog) became *Canis familiaris*.

1. Simia Simia
2. Ursus Ursus
3. Leo Leo
4. Tigris Tigris
5. Felis Felis
6. Mustela Mustela
7. Lutra Lutra
8. Hyaena Hyaena
9. Canis Canis
10. Talpa Talpa
11. Vespertilio Vespertilio
12. Hystrix Hystrix
13. Sciurus Sciurus
14. Mus Mus
15. Lepus Lepus
16. Sorex Sorex
17. Equus Equus
18. Elephas Elephas
19. Sus Sus
20. Cervus Cervus
21. Ovis Ovis
22. Bos Bos
23. Psittacus Psittacus
24. Falco Falco
25. Corvus Corvus
26. Cuculus Cuculus
27. Picus Picus
28. Certhia Certhia
29. Upupa Upupa
30. Ispida Ispida
31. Grus Grus
32. Ciconia Ciconia
33. Ardea Ardea
34. Anas Anas
35. Mergus Mergus
36. Graculus Graculus
37. Colymbus Colymbus
38. Larus Larus
39. Tringa Tringa
40. Pavo Pavo
41. Gallina Gallina
42. Tetrao Tetrao
43. Columba Columba
44. Turdus Turdus
45. Sturnus Sturnus
46. Alauda Alauda
47. Motacilla Motacilla
48. Luscinia Luscinia
49. Parus Parus
50. Hirundo Hirundo
51. Loxia Loxia
52. Fringilla Fringilla
53. Testudo Testudo
54. Rana Rana

55. Anguis Anguis
56. Balaena Balaena
57. Delphinus Delphinus
58. Raja Raja
59. Ostracion Ostracion
60. Cottus Cottus
61. Perca Perca
62. Sparus Sparus
63. Mugil Mugil
64. Scomber Scomber
65. Gobius Gobius
66. Blennus Blennus
67. Ammodytes Ammodytes
68. Salmo Salmo
69. Cyprinus Cyprinus
70. Blatta Blatta
71. Curculio Curculio
72. Cantharis Cantharis
73. Papilio Papilio
74. Apis Apis
75. Ichneumon Ichneumon
76. Gryllus Gryllus
77. Formica Formica
78. Cimex Cimex
79. Notonecta Notonecta
80. Scorpio Scorpio
81. Pediculus Pediculus
82. Pulex Pulex
83. Monoculus Monoculus
84. Araneus Araneus
85. Cancer Cancer
86. Scolopendria Scolopendria
87. Lumbricus Lumbricus
88. Limax Limax
89. Cochlea Cochlea
90. Nautilus Nautilus
91. Patella Patella
92. Dentalium Dentalium
93. Echinus Echinus
94. Sepia Sepia

SELECT ETYMOLOGIES

tautonym: from the Greek words "tauto," meaning "the same," and "onoma," meaning "name." Related words include "tautology," "synonym," "antonym," and "homonym."

binomial nomenclature: from the Latin words "bis," "nomen," and "calare," meaning essentially "two name name-calling (system)." The term "binomial nomenclature" is used in botany, but the technically correct term in zoology is the slightly different "binominal nomenclature," which has the same meaning and a nearly identical etymology. Nevertheless, "binomial nomenclature" is often used in zoology and its meaning is commonly understood.

taxonomy: from the Greek words "taxis," meaning "arrangement," and "nomia" meaning "custom." Taxonomy is the study of general principles of scientific classification, including the orderly classification of plants and animals according to their natural relationships.

etymology: from the Greek word "etymologia," meaning essentially, "analysis of a word to find its true origin," from "etymon" for "true sense," and "logia" for "study of."

SPECIES CONCEPTS

A common query concerns how scientists determine whether two organisms are part of the same or different species. This topic is too complex to be covered here, suffice to say that there is a rich academic discussion of this issue with biologists advocating for different definitions of what constitutes a species. These definitions are known as species concepts. In many instances, species concepts are incompatible with each other, difficult or impossible to test, or useful for some groups of animals but not others. Some of the most well-known species concepts examine whether organisms can naturally reproduce with each other to create viable and fertile offspring, whether organisms are part of a single lineage throughout space and time with its own evolutionary tendencies and history, and whether organisms have similar morphological characteristics that distinguish them from other organisms. There are many other species concepts, and no single concept has been universally accepted as the definitive answer to the species problem.

BOTANICAL AND BACTERIOLOGICAL TAUTONYMS, AND A PROPOSAL TO REVISE ICNAFP RECOMMENDATION 60F.1 AND ARTICLE 23.4

Rules of botanical nomenclature are set forth in the *International Code of Nomenclature for algae, fungi, and plants*; rules of bacteriological nomenclature are set forth in the *International Code of Nomenclature of Prokaryotes*; and rules of zoological nomenclature are set forth in the *International Code of Zoological Nomenclature*. The names of these codes have changed over time, and for the sake of simplicity and the benefit of a lay audience, the discussion that follows will refer to them as the botanical nomenclature code, the bacteriological nomenclature code, and the zoological nomenclature code, respectively. Specific versions of each code will be referred to by year.

History of Tautonyms Prohibitions. As noted in Part I, rules of botanical nomenclature forbid tautonyms when naming algae, fungi, and plants, stating that "[t]he specific epithet . . . may not exactly repeat the generic name (a designation formed by such repetition is a tautonym)." The reason for this rule is not expressly stated in the code, and there is no such rule in zoology. There have been many versions of the botanical nomenclature code with the earliest versions from 1867 and 1883 making no reference to tautonyms. The first prohibition of tautonyms appears in the 1906 version where it is said that "[s]pecific names must also be rejected . . . [w]hen they merely repeat the generic name." Examples of impermissible tautonyms are provided in the 1906 version, but reasons for this rule are not. This rule is found in every version of the botanical nomenclature code since 1906, with the word "tautonym" first appearing in the 1935 version: "Specific epithets are illegitimate . . . and must be rejected . . . [w]hen they exactly repeat the generic name with or without the addition of a transcribed symbol (tautonym)." Again, examples are given but reasons for the rule are not. The same is true of the current botanical nomenclature code, published in 2018.

The history of tautonym permissibility in bacteriological nomenclature is slightly more interesting and perhaps more informative. One of the first proposed codes of nomenclature for bacteria, published in 1947, stated that specific epithets are illegitimate and must be rejected "[w]hen they exactly repeat the generic name (Tautonym)." The phrasing of this rule is nearly identical to the tautonym prohibition in botanical nomenclature at the time, and it appeared again in 1948 and 1958 versions of the bacteriological nomenclature code. However, the prohibition of tautonyms was dropped from the bacteriological nomenclature code as of the 1975 version, and it did not appear in either the 1990 version or the current, 2008 version. Therefore, tautonyms are permissible for bacteria and other prokaryotes governed by the 2008 code. That said, there are still sources being published today that repeat without citation the now-outdated rule that tautonyms are strictly forbidden for bacteria.

The reason for prohibiting tautonyms in the earlier versions of the bacteriological nomenclature code is not entirely clear. Those early codes cited certain "principles" when stating the rule against tautonyms, but those principles do not clearly explain why tautonymous names are problematic or against the purposes of the code. The most on-point principle cited in the rule against bacteriological tautonyms, "Principle 1," recommended avoiding names "which may cause error or ambiguity or throw science into confusion." When this rule was written, however, tautonyms had already existed in zoology for many decades without "throwing science into confusion," so the rationale for this rule seems somewhat unpersuasive—at least, without more information.

The history of tautonyms in zoological nomenclature is also interesting. The 1878 zoological nomenclature code prohibited tautonyms because they were considered "inelegan[t]," but no further explanation as to why they were seen as inelegant was provided. Presumably, tautonyms were disfavored because their specific epithets failed to "express some distinguishing characteristic of the [animal] to which they are applied," which was considered a desirable quality and a reflection of "[t]he *best* zoological names." At that time, scientific names of animals were not only unique identifiers as they are today, but also tools of communicating something about the morphology, habitat, distribution, or behavior of the animals to which they referred. The 1905 version of the zoological nomenclature code was quick to change course and state unequivocally that "[a] name is not to be rejected because of tautonymy, that is, because the specific or the specific and subspecific names are identical with the generic name." Tautonyms have been allowed in zoology ever since. Of note, the 1878 zoological nomenclature code also recommended against the use of "nonsense names," anagrams, "corrupted words," compound words composed of two different languages, words of more than five syllables, and other types of words as being "inelegant," "great deformities," or "as deformed a monster in nomenclature as a Mermaid or a Centaur would be in zoology." These recommendations have also since been repealed in zoology.

In terms of other nomenclature codes, tautonyms are prohibited by the code of nomenclature for cultivated plants, but they are not prohibited by the code of nomenclature for viruses.

Epithet Capitalization as the Reason to Prohibit Tautonyms. A working hypothesis on the reason for the botanical and bacteriological rules against tautonyms is that prior versions of those nomenclature codes had now-outdated rules on taxon name capitalization that could have allowed tautonymous names to cause confusion. In particular, earlier nomenclature codes for botany and bacteria allowed specific epithets to begin with capital letters when the epithets were derived from the names of persons, or in some instances, from the names of current or former genera. This position on capitalization first appears in the 1906 botanical nomenclature code and was included in many subsequent versions of that code. In the absence of a rule against tautonyms, this capitalization practice would have allowed plant or bacteria names like *Rex Rex*, where the specific epithet is derived from the name of the illustrator of this book. The position on capitalization in the botanical nomenclature code was eventually revised 100 years later in the 2006 version, which removed the carve-out for names of persons, etc., and simply recommended that initial lowercase letters be used for all specific epithets: "All specific and infraspecific epithets should be written with an initial lower-case letter." This new recommendation remains in force in the current, 2018 version of the botanical nomenclature code.

The capitalization rule is important to the tautonyms issue because two words that are identical in spelling and capitalization can be mistaken for each other in certain contexts. Using the example above, a reference simply to the taxon "*Rex*," without more, would be ambiguous as to whether the intended reference is the genus *Rex* or the specific epithet *Rex*. Indeed, the examples of prohibited tautonyms in the 1906 version of the botanical nomenclature code are *Linaria Linaria* and *Raphanistrum Raphanistrum*—both of which are identical not just in spelling but also in capitalization. So it seems that the origins of the rule prohibiting tautonyms lie in concerns about confusion of words that are both identically spelled and identically capitalized. Use of initial lowercase letters in specific epithets, as is now recommended in all instances in botanical nomenclature, avoids any potential for confusion between "*Rex*" and "*rex*," or "*Linaria*" and "*linaria*," because the capitalized word indicates the generic name, and the lowercase word indicates the specific epithet.

The capitalization rules in bacteriological nomenclature have a slightly different history, which appears to support the view that the prohibition of tautonyms is a result of permitting epithet capitalization. The Foreword to the 1947 proposed bacteriological nomenclature code noted that bacteriologists were aware of, and generally in agreement with, the existing rule in botany that specific epithets should begin with lowercase letters except when they are derived from names of persons. However, early versions of the bacteriological nomenclature code also contained the following recommendation: "Specific epithets, even those derived from names of persons, should not be capitalized." This recommendation was elevated to a rule in the same edition of the bacteriological code (1975) that also removed the rule against tautonyms. The difference between a recommendation and a rule is important because, per the code, a name that is contrary to a rule is invalid and must be rejected, but a name that is contrary to a mere recommendation cannot be rejected on that basis. Recommendations do not have the force of rules and "deal with subsidiary points." The 1975 capitalization rule—Rule 59—states: "An epithet, even one derived from the name of a person, should not be written with an initial capital letter." This same rule was included in the 1990 and 2008 versions of the bacteriological nomenclature code, which as noted above, also do not prohibit tautonyms. The result of this change is that all specific epithets of bacteria must begin with a lowercase letter.

To summarize the timeline of relevant revisions to the bacteriological nomenclature code: When capitalization of specific epithets was allowed (despite recommendations to the contrary), tautonyms were prohibited. When capitalization of specific epithets was prohibited, the rule against tautonyms was repealed. In other words, versions of the bacteriological nomenclature code either allow epithet capitalization, or they allow tautonyms, but not both. Again, this makes sense because a specific epithet and a generic name that are identical in spelling and capitalization (*Rex Rex*) could lead to confusion, but any difference in spelling or capitalization would make each word unique (*Rex rex*).

One might argue that the timing of the bacteriological nomenclature rule changes for capitalization and tautonyms are merely coincidental and do not have an established causal relationship. This is a fair point, but the history of the capitalization rule in the zoological nomenclature code is informative. One of the first written zoological nomenclature codes was drafted by zoologists in 1842 and published the following year. That first code anticipated the very problem described above, and it adopted the very same lowercase-epithet requirement to resolve that problem:

Specific names to be written with a small initial.

A convenient *memoria technica* may be effected by adopting our next proposition. It has been usual, when the titles of species are derived from proper names, to write them with a capital letter, and hence when the specific name is used alone it is liable to be occasionally mistaken for the title of a genus. But if the titles of *species* were *invariably* written with a *small* initial, and those of *genera* with a *capital*, the eye would at once distinguish the rank of the group referred to, and a possible source of error would be avoided. It should be further remembered that all species are *equal*, and should therefore be written all *alike*. We suggest, then, that

§ C. Specific names should *always* be written with a small initial letter, even when derived from persons or places, and generic names should be always written with a capital.

This tends to confirm that confusion in taxonomic rank caused by epithet capitalization was a concern among taxonomists in the mid-19th century—a problem that would have been exacerbated by tautonymous names. It is curious that the botanical nomenclature codes of 1906 and later did not adopt a similar rule, despite the rule existing in zoology for many decades prior. In any event, as noted above, the zoological nomenclature code has allowed tautonyms for well-over a century, perhaps due in part to its longstanding requirement that specific epithets (technically known as "specific names" in zoology) begin with lowercase letters.

<u>Proposed Revisions to the Botanical Nomenclature Code.</u> Having reviewed the histories of all three nomenclature codes, a pattern emerges: When specific epithets must begin with lowercase letters, tautonyms are permitted. When specific epithets may begin with capital letters, tautonyms are prohibited. With this in mind, it appears that the current prohibition of tautonyms in botany is a vestige of prior versions of the botanical nomenclature code, and that the rules and customs that gave rise to the tautonym prohibition largely no longer exist.

As noted, the current botanical nomenclature code contains a recommendation that all specific epithets be written with initial lowercase letters. Although this recommendation does not have the force of a rule, it is the widely prevailing custom—perhaps even a universal custom today—that specific epithets in botany begin with lowercase letters. The International Botanical Congress should consider elevating this longstanding and much-observed recommendation (60F.1) to the status of a rule (*i.e.*, an "Article"). Doing so would have limited, if any, practical impact on botanical nomenclature given its already widespread adoption and the fact that it is a mere typographical change. The good reasons for this change were persuasively articulated by zoologists in 1842, as provided above. In conjunction with this change, the Congress should also consider wholly or partially repealing the rule prohibiting tautonyms (Article 23.4). Such a change has proven to be workable in both bacteriological and zoological nomenclature when combined with the requirement that specific epithets begin with lowercase letters.

Any retroactive application of such rule changes would have a limited impact on botanical nomenclature given that tautonymous names have been prohibited for so much of botanical taxonomic history and few names, if any, would require retroactive revision based on priority or otherwise. Non-retroactive application of these changes would eliminate complicated naming problems that arise when species are reclassified to genera that bear the same name as their specific epithet (*e.g.*, transferring *Linum radiola* to the *Radiola* genus) and would preserve the epithets that were originally assigned. These rule changes would also help to simplify and streamline the code by resulting in one less, now-unnecessary rule. Indeed, the avoidance of the useless creation of names is a goal of the code, and so too should be the avoidance of the useless creation of rules.

Finally, although botanical tradition has shunned tautonyms, permitting them may perhaps inspire greater public interest and academic enthusiasm in botanical taxonomy and nomenclature, the fruits of which could be substantial at a time when reports indicate a steady decline in both students entering the field of taxonomy and in university resources devoted to relevant courses and collections. Whether it ought to be so or not, tautonyms are a matter of popular curiosity, with numerous popular websites and articles dedicated to the subject. They also make memorization of scientific names easier for children and other non-botanists or non-zoologists, acting as a gateway to taxonomy. These facts, trivial though they may seem to experts in the field, might encourage a new generation to pursue careers in botanical taxonomy at this critical time of climate change and human alteration of our natural world. Should the Congress have doubts about this proposal, an alternative proposal that would still improve the code would be to promote the capitalization recommendation to a rule as discussed, and to demote the rule against tautonyms to a recommendation rather than eliminating it entirely. The result of this is similar in that it requires lowercase initial letters in specific epithets and also allows, but discourages, tautonyms. At a minimum, and putting tautonyms aside, the Congress should consider elevating the capitalization recommendation to a rule as has been done with good reason in bacteriological and zoological nomenclature codes.

A concise, much abridged version of these arguments and historical observations has been published in the international taxonomy journal *Taxon* (Volume 72, Issue 2, Apr. 2023), and has been submitted for consideration to the Nomenclature Section of the XX International Botanical Congress. The Congress will vote on this proposal when it convenes in Madrid, Spain in July 2024.

ABOUT THE AUTHOR

***Michael J. Stephan* — Tautonyms author.** This mammal can be found in southern California, often running trails, playing guitar, or researching incredibly specific and random topics in silence for hours on end and for no apparent reason. His last name is derived from the Greek word "stephanos," meaning "that which surrounds" or "crown." He has a mutualistic relationship with a *Canis familiaris* named Moonshine.

All proceeds received by the author from the sale of this book are donated to wildlife charities.